SO-ABA-946

Out With DOUBT

A Look at the Evidence for Christianity

Kyle Butt, M.A.

APOLOGETICS PRESS

Apologetics Press, Inc.
230 Landmark Drive
Montgomery, Alabama 36117-2752

© Copyright 2001
ISBN-10: 0-932859-43-7
ISBN-13: 978-0-932859-43-3
Printed in China

Library of Congress Cataloging-in-Publication

Butt, Kyle, 1976 -

Out Wit Doubt: A Look at the Evidence for Christianity / Kyle Butt

Includes bibliographic references and subject, name, and Scripture indices.

ISBN-10: 0-932859-43-7
ISBN-13: 978-0-932859-43-3

1. Creation. 2. Science and religion. 3. Apologetics and polemics. I. Title

213—dc21   00-135278

DEDICATION

To Bethany, my wife—a lady who has made it easy for me to realize why the Bible says, "He who finds a wife finds a good thing" (Proverbs 18:22).

TABLE OF CONTENTS

FOREWORD

Tommy couldn't remember any teacher as cool as Mr. Hinson. Mr. Hinson was 28 years old, single, and drove a brand new convertible sports car. He coached junior high boys' basketball, and taught seventh and eighth grade science and social studies. All the girls thought he was cute. He had just graduated with a Master's degree in science, and was the smartest person Tommy had ever met. Well, almost the smartest. Tommy's dad was really smart about some things like building houses and repairing dishwashers; but Mr. Hinson knew science. In fact, he could answer every question any student ever asked. He knew—right off the top of his head—that the Earth is 93 million miles from the Sun. He knew that the human body has exactly 206 bones in it, and that the average human brain weighs 2.2 pounds.

Not only that, Mr. Hinson knew all about dinosaurs. He knew where they lived, what they looked like, and which ones were the biggest and ate the most. Every day in Mr. Hinson's class was different. Sometimes the class would do experiments and make aspirin or Nylon from bottled chemicals in the lab. Other days, Hinson (he told the class that they did not have to call him Mr.) would take them outside to examine different tree leaves and types of grasses. Tommy really thought Mr. Hinson was a great teacher, and all his friends agreed.

But Tommy had one big problem. Mr. Hinson taught some things about the Universe that Tommy had not been taught at home. For instance, when he taught the unit on dinosaurs, he said that some of their bones were around 150 million years old. And when he explained about the meat-eating Venus Flytrap, he said that it just happened by genetic mutations and natural selection. None of those things really bothered Tommy until today.

Today in Mr. Hinson's science class was different because he talked about God, or to state it more correctly, the idea that there is no God.

"Today class," said Mr. Hinson, "we are going to talk about the origin of the Universe. Who can tell me how it got here?" Eugene Lepton, the class genius who read his science textbook for fun, said, "It started out as a tiny, dense ball about the size of a period at the end of a sentence. Then it exploded in what is called the 'Big Bang' and sent particles flying all over. Eventually the planets organized in orbits." "Very good," Hinson commended, "That's exactly right." "Now, can anyone tell me how old the Universe is?" Lucy Landsdale, who always tried to outdo Eugene, piped up: "Most scientists say that the Universe is about 8 to 20 billion years old." "Right again," said Mr. Hinson. "And how did life originate on our planet Earth?" This time nobody answered, so Mr. Hinson began to explain. "Hundreds of millions of years ago, in a chemical swamp, a single-celled organism formed from nonliving compounds. It genetically mutated and evolved into multicellular bacteria. Those bacteria adapted and evolved through more mutations and natural selection, and then changed into different types of plants and animals. Eventually, mammals like apes and monkeys evolved, and we humans evolved from a common ancestor that we shared with them."

Suddenly, Jimmy Johnson—whose dad preached at a large church in town—blurted out in a rather nervous-sounding voice: "That is not true. The Bible says that God created the whole Universe in six days, and created man out of the dust of the Earth." Tommy knew he had been taught that same thing about God, and he silently wished that he had the courage to do what Jimmy was doing.

Mr. Hinson chuckled and said: "Yes, Jimmy that is what the Bible says," as he walked over to his desk and pulled a black Bible from the top drawer. He read several verses from Genesis about God creating the whole Universe. The Bible was a King James Version, and many of the words sounded weird to the class. Then Mr. Hinson continued: "You see, the Bible is an old book filled with old ideas and lots of mistakes. Very few really smart people believe the Bible anymore. In fact, modern science has proven that many of the things in the Bible simply cannot be true. If a loving God, like the Bible describes, really does exist, He would not allow innocent people like children to die."

Tommy was filled with doubt and terribly confused. If what Mr. Hinson taught was true, then there was no God Who created the Earth, and all those lessons he had learned in Bible class about the days of Creation, Adam and Eve, and even stories about Jesus, were not true.

But how could Mr. Hinson be wrong about this part of science; he knew a lot more about science than anyone Tommy had ever met.

Tommy was faced with the problem that every one of us already has faced or someday will face—He doubted his belief in God and the Bible. As we grow and mature, new ideas and alternative theories come our way. What are we to do with all the conflicting thoughts and opinions? The apostle Paul gave us the answer in 1 Thessalonians 5:21 when he wrote: "Test all things; hold fast to that which is good."

Faith in God is not something that your parents, your preacher, or your friends can hand to you on a silver platter (although they can be helpful). Faith is something that **you** must work hard to obtain. It does not come easily, and along the way many conflicting concepts will try to hinder your progress. However, if you will test all things, you will find that faith in God stands the test.

This book is designed to lead young people toward a stronger faith in God by providing concrete evidence that establishes the existence of God, the infallibility of the Bible, and the truthfulness of Creation. Everyone has to choose what he or she will believe. The purpose of this book is to help its readers cast out doubts that come with maturing knowledge and development.

Kyle Butt

"Before the mountains were brought forth, or ever You had formed the Earth and the world, even from everlasting to everlasting, You are God."

Psalm 90:2

After all, one ape never sat around and said to another, "Today I think we should talk about right and wrong."

DOES GOD EXIST?
— Part 1 —

One of the most basic questions that each human being must answer is, "Does God exist?" Let's face it—either God exists, or He doesn't. There is no middle ground. The only way to answer this question is to examine the evidence. Surely it is reasonable to suggest that **if** there is a God, He would make available enough evidence to prove His existence. Does such evidence exist?

CAUSE AND EFFECT

The Universe is here, and is real. Every rational person acknowledges this point. If the Universe did not exist, we wouldn't be here to talk about it. So the question arises, "How did the Universe get here?" There are only three choices: (1) it is eternal (meaning it always has been and always will be here); (2) it created itself; or (3) it was created. If it isn't eternal, and if it didn't create itself, then obviously it must have had a cause.

Let's consider the Law of Cause and Effect. As far as science knows, natural laws have no exceptions. This definitely is true of the Law of Cause and Effect, which is the most universal and most certain of all laws. Simply put, the Law of Cause and Effect states that every material effect must have an adequate cause that existed before the effect ("material" refers to anything composed of matter or energy).

Material effects without adequate causes do not exist. Also, causes never occur after the effect. In addition, the effect never is greater than the cause, which is why scientists state that every material effect must have an **adequate** cause. The river didn't turn muddy because the frog jumped in; the book didn't fall off the table because the fly landed on it. These are not adequate causes. For whatever effects we see, we must present adequate causes.

Five-year-olds are terrific at using the Law of Cause and Effect. We can picture a small child asking: "Mommy, where do peaches come from?" Her mother would say that they come from peach trees. Then the child might ask where the trees come from, and her mother might say they come from peaches. You can see the cycle. Eventually, the child wants to know how the first peach tree got here. She can see that it must have had a cause, and she wants to know what that cause was.

One thing is for sure, the Universe did not create itself. We recognize this as a scientific fact, because matter cannot create matter. If we take a rock that weighs one pound and do 50,000 experiments on it, we never will be able to produce any more rock than we already have. So, whatever caused the Universe could not have been material.

From Nothing Comes Nothing

I know that it is insulting to your intelligence to have to include this paragraph, but some people today are saying that the Universe came into being from nothing; that matter simply created itself. However, if there ever had been a time when absolutely nothing existed, then there would be nothing now, because it always is true that nothing produces nothing. (If something exists now, then something always has existed.)

Morality and Mankind

As we continue to discuss things in this Universe that require a cause, we must include the fact that all humans have some kind of moral code. Everyone in the world believes that certain things are right, while other things are wrong. At times, people may not agree on the exact way to decide whether something is right or wrong. But it is undeniable that the concepts of right and wrong, good and evil, do exist.

The person who does not believe that God exists has only one choice when it comes to explaining morality —man must have thought it up by himself. However, since man is seen as little more than the last animal to be produced by evolution, this becomes a problem. A lion does not feel guilty after killing a gazelle for lunch. A dog does not feel remorse after stealing a bone from another dog. And a female pig feels no guilt after eating her newborn piglets. Yet man, who is supposed to have evolved, feels both guilt and remorse when he commits certain acts that violate his moral code. The simple fact that we even discuss morals proves that morality—which is found only in humans—had to have a cause. After all, one ape never sat around and said to another, "Today, I think we should talk about right and wrong." Even the famous atheist George Gaylord Simpson of Harvard University said that "morals arise only in man." What—or should we say **Who**—is responsible for man's morality?

The Bible Speaks About the Cause

The Bible certainly is not silent about what caused the Universe. In the very first verse of the first chapter of the first book, it records: "In the beginning God created the heavens and the Earth." Acts 17:24 states: "God, who made the world and everything in it. . .He is Lord of heaven and earth." Exodus 20:11 notes: "For in six days the Lord made the heavens and the earth, the sea, and all that is in them."

God is undoubtedly an adequate cause, since He is all-powerful. In Genesis 17:1, God told Abraham "I am **Almighty** God."

God existed long before this material world in which we live, thus fulfilling the criterion that the cause must come before the effect. The psalmist wrote: "Before the mountains were brought forth, or ever You had formed the earth and the world, even from everlasting to everlasting, You are God" (Psalm 90:2).

And He definitely would be expected to instill within mankind the important concept of morality, since He is a God of morals. For example, when the apostle Paul wrote to Titus, he spoke of "God, who cannot lie" (Titus 1:2).

Only God fits the criteria of an adequate cause that came before the Universe.

Why Does God not Have a Cause?

Hold on just a minute! If we contend that every material effect must have a cause, and we say that only God could have caused the Universe, then the obvious question is: "What caused God?" Doesn't the Law of Cause and Effect apply to God, too?

There is a single word in the Law of Cause and Effect that helps provide the answer to this question—the word **material**. Every **material** effect must have a cause that existed before it. Scientists formulated the Law of Cause and Effect based upon what they have observed while studying this Universe, which is composed of matter and energy. No science experiment in the world can be performed on God, because He is an eternal spirit—not matter (John 4:24). Science is far from learning everything about this material world, and it is even farther from understanding the eternal nature of God. There had to be a first Cause, and God was (and is) the only One suitable for the job.

CONCLUSION

The Law of Cause and Effect is a scientifically established law that does not have any known exceptions. It was not conjured up from a magic hat to prove the existence of God, although it does that quite well. The evidence in this chapter is sufficient to show that this material Universe needs a non-material cause. That non-material Cause is God. If natural forces created the Universe, randomly selecting themselves, then morality in humans never could be explained. Why is this Universe here? Because "In the beginning, God...."

DISCUSSION QUESTIONS

1. Discuss what society would be like if it were based on the evolutionary principle of "survival of the fittest." Compare your answers to Psalm 14. How have morals in humans affected society?

2. Think of anything else, other than God, which would represent an adequate cause for this magnificent Universe. What are some things other people have said could have caused the Universe? Now compare the results with the concept of God. Which one makes better sense?

3. What are some moral concepts that are practically the same in all humans? Why do you think these moral concepts are virtually universal? Use Genesis 1:26, Exodus 20:1-17, Titus 1:2, and Romans 2:6 to help formulate your answer.

4. Why would some people want to say that the Universe created itself out of nothing? If God does exist, how **should** that change people's lives? However, if it could be shown that God does not exist, how would that affect human behavior?

5. How long has God existed? Discuss the concept of eternity. What is the difference between a being that is eternal and one that is immortal?

"For since the creation of the world His invisible attributes are clearly seen, being understood by the things that are made, even His everlasting power and divinity, that they may be without excuse."

Romans 1:20

The Universe is huge, well designed, and runs more efficiently than clock-work.

DOES GOD EXIST?
— Part 2 —

It is no secret that everything designed must have a designer—every poem a poet, every painting a painter. Even an atheist cannot argue with this idea. If you were to walk through the forest and see a shiny, new convertible sitting amidst the trees, you obviously would think that an intelligent designer had created it and put it there. No rational person would believe that natural forces accidentally and randomly formed the car.

DESIGN DEMANDS A DESIGNER

Those who believe in God often use this argument to establish the fact that since the Universe shows design, it must have had a designer. While the atheist admits that all design demands a designer, he will not admit that there is design in the Universe. He may agree that there is complexity, orderliness, and precision, but he will not admit that there is design. Therefore, in order to establish the fact that an intelligent designer exists, we must show that the natural world exhibits more than simple orderliness or complexity. So, for the rest of this chapter we will take a walk through the "Design Hall of Fame."

It's Not a Small World After All

Have you ever gone outside on a clear summer evening and looked up into the night sky? What a beautiful sight—with all the shining, twinkling stars. Scientists tell us that we can see about 3,000 stars just by using our eyes. But if we use a simple telescope, we can see over 100,000 stars!

Our Universe, however, has many more stars than that. Astronomers suggest that it has over 25 sextillion stars in it (that's the number 25, followed by 21 zeros!). They also say it contains over one billion galaxies, each of which has around 100 billion individual stars.

The Universe is so large that scientists determine distances within it by measuring how long it takes light to travel from one place to another. Light moves so fast that it can go about 186,000 miles in one second. That means in a year, light can go almost six trillion miles— a distance known as one light-year.

The diameter of the Milky Way Galaxy (in which our solar system and Earth are located) is 100,000 light-years across. This means that even if you had a spaceship that could travel at the speed of light, it still would take 100,000 years to go across our galaxy (during which time you would travel over 587 quadrillion miles, and you still would have been through only one of the billion galaxies!). If you somehow were able to travel across the entire Universe, astronomers say it would take about 20 billion years—even traveling at the speed of light.

It's no wonder that David said: "The heavens declare the glory of God; and the firmament shows His handiwork" (Psalm 19:1).

Even Though It's Big, It's Not Clumsy

While the size of the Universe is impressive, its design is even more spectacular. When we examine the facts, it is obvious that God designed it for us. The Earth is 93 million miles from the Sun—a distance that happens to be just right for life to exist. The Sun is like a giant furnace. It gives off more energy in a single second than mankind has produced since the Creation. It converts 8 million tons of matter into energy every single second, and has an interior temperature of more than 20 million degrees Celsius. If the Earth were even slightly closer to this wonderful star, people could not live because of the horrible heat and radiation. Interestingly, as the Earth moves in its elliptical orbit around the Sun, it departs from a straight line by only one-ninth of an inch every eighteen miles. If it departed by one-eighth of an inch, we would come so close to the Sun that we would burn up; if it departed by one-tenth of an inch, we would freeze to death.[*]

Also, the Earth has exactly the right surface temperature. The mean global temperature on the Earth is 11.3° Celsius (about 57° Fahrenheit[**]), which is perfectly suitable for human, animal, and plant life. But the average temperature on Pluto is a freezing -230°C, and on Venus it is a scalding 480°C! Nothing can grow in these extremely low or extremely high temperatures.

---

[*] *Science Digest*, 1981, 89[1]:124, January/February.

[**] *Time*, 2001, 157[14]:23, April 9.

The Earth is slanted on its axis at precisely 23.5 degrees. If it were not tilted, but instead sat straight up in its orbit around the Sun, there would be no seasons as we know them. The tropics would be hotter, and the deserts would get bigger. If the tilt went all the way over to 90 degrees, much of the Earth would alternate between very cold winters and very hot summers.

The Moon is 240,000 miles from the Earth. This, too, is just right, since the Moon helps control movement of ocean tides. This movement is beneficial to the Earth, because it provides a cleansing of shorelines and helps ocean life prosper. Without such tides, water in the oceans would stagnate, and the animals and plants living in them would die. Our existence on Earth depends on the Moon being just the right distance from the Earth.

Earth's oceans are another good example of perfect design. Water covers approximately 72% of the Earth's surface, which is good because the oceans provide a reservoir of moisture that constantly evaporates and condenses. Eventually, this causes rain to fall on the Earth. It is a well-known fact that water heats and cools at a much slower rate than a solid land mass, which explains why deserts can be blistering hot in the daytime and yet freezing cold at night. But water holds its temperature longer, and thus provides a natural heating and cooling system for land areas on Earth. The Earth's average temperature is maintained in large part by the heat reserves found within the waters of the oceans.

Another well-known fact is that humans and many animals breathe in oxygen and breathe out carbon dioxide. Plants, on the other hand, take in carbon dioxide and give off oxygen. Humans and animals depend on the plant world for a constant, fresh supply of oxygen. But approximately 50% of all oxygen comes from tiny, microscopic plants within the Earth's oceans and seas.

The Universe is huge, well designed, and runs more efficiently than clockwork. The Earth is the right distance from the Sun; it is exactly the right distance from the Moon; it has exactly the right tilt on its axis; it has exactly the right amount of oxygen. Countless other conditions are exactly right as well. Could all these things be "just right" by accident?

The Eyes Have It

The human eye is one of the most complicated mechanisms in the world. Even Charles Darwin said that it is hard to believe that this magnificent device could arise accidentally. The eye gathers over 80% of the knowledge that is transmitted to the brain. The brain is connected to each eye by over 600,000 nerves that send it messages at a speed exceeding 300 miles an hour! Scientists tell us that the eye receives 1.5 million messages at the same time, sorts through them, and sends them to the brain. The retina covers less than a square inch, and contains 137 million light-sensitive receptor cells, 130 million rods (allowing the eye to see in black and white), and 7 million cones (allowing the eye to see in full color). On any given day, the eye may move about 100,000 times, using muscles that, milligram for milligram, are among the body's strongest. The body would have to walk 50 miles to exercise the leg muscles an equal amount. The eye is self-cleaning. Lacrimal glands produce tears to flush away dust and other foreign materials. Eyelids act as windshield washers. The blinking process (3-6 times a minute) keeps the sensitive cornea moist and clean. And tears contain a potent microbe-killer (lysozyme) that guards the eyes against bacterial infection. During times of stress, one eye will rest while the other does 90% of the work; then the process is reversed, allowing both eyes equal amounts of relaxation.[*]

In fact, the eye works so well that technological companies model cameras after it. Today, we have tiny camcorders that can be held in one hand and be used in both bright and dim light. They have lenses, automatic focus, color monitors, and other well-engineered features that allow them to record images. Yet, even with all the time, effort, and money that went into designing these technological jewels, they are but clumsy replicas of the human eye. If we found a camcorder lying on the ground, who among us would suggest that it "just happened" by chance? Yet the average human being has two eyes that make the camcorder look like a kindergarten toy. If we are looking for design, truly the eyes have it.

The Nature of Nature

Even though the Universe and human eye both show intricate design, they are by no means the only places to look for God's handiwork. The following examples of design in nature not only are intriguing, but also provide good evidence of a Designer.

A Bird With a Thermometer

We all remember having our temperature taken when we were sick. Sometimes we had to hold the thermom-

---

[*] Ratcliff, J.D. (1980), *I Am Joe's Body* (New York: Reader's Digest Association/Berkley Books), pp. 25-29.

eter under our tongue for a whole minute. As technology advanced, new thermometers were created that could be inserted into the ear, taking only a few seconds to measure temperature. But there is an Australian bird called the mallee fowl that has a built-in thermometer far more accurate than the ones used to measure a human's temperature.

When the time comes for the female mallee fowl to lay her eggs, the male bird digs a pit in the ground and piles a large mound of sticks and leaves in it. He covers this pile with sand, sometimes making it as tall as four feet. With the sand on top, the leaves and sticks begin to rot, which produces heat. The male makes a hole in the top of the mound where the female lays one egg. About a week later he will make another hole and she will lay another egg. This process goes on until there are about 18 eggs in the nest.

Several times every day, the male pokes his beak into the mound. He sticks out his tongue, which is such a good thermometer that it can measure a temperature change of 1/10 of a degree. If the mound is too hot, he removes some of the sand. If it is too cool, he adds more. The baby birds hatch after about seven weeks.

How does the mallee fowl know the exact temperature for the eggs, or that rotting leaves covered by sand will produce heat? And why is it that his tongue can measure temperature changes of 1/10 of a degree? For one simple reason: the mallee fowl is well designed.

A Beetle With a Big Bang

The bombardier beetle is a little creature that packs a big punch. He has two storage chambers, one on each side of his body. In one chamber he keeps hydrogen peroxide (yes, it's the same stuff that your parents put on a scraped knee—except stronger) and chemicals known as hydroquinones. In the other chamber, he stores enzymes (proteins that speed up chemical reactions). When the two are kept separated, they are perfectly harmless. But if an enemy attacks the little fellow, he empties the two chemicals into a central chamber within his body.

As a result of this mixing process, the chemicals form liquids and gases that heat up to 212°F (the boiling point of water). The beetle takes aim with two small, gun-like projections on the rear of his body and fires the boiling mixture into the face of his attacker. Boom! The caustic chemicals shoot out, the enemy is thwarted, and the little beetle goes on his way.

Only intelligent design can explain how the beetle is able to produce the proper chemicals, keep them separate until they are needed for his defense, and then propel the explosive mixture into the face of his enemy.

CONCLUSION

Truly, the design found in the Universe, the human eye, and nature is sufficient to reveal the hand of a designer. The apostle Paul wrote in Romans 1:20: "For since the creation of the world His invisible attributes are clearly seen, being understood by the things that are made, even His everlasting power and divinity, that they may be without excuse." Every watch has a watchmaker; every painting has a painter; every building has a builder; but "He who built all things is God" (Hebrews 3:4).

DISCUSSION QUESTIONS

1. Discuss how the size of the Universe dwarfs individual people. How does God view humans? Use the following verses to help in the discussion: Matthew 10:27-31, Mark 8:36-38, Genesis 1:28.

2. List some other things that show definite design. Why did God make the Universe so complex and beautiful? One reason can be found in 1 Timothy 6:17 and Ecclesiastes 5:18-19; Psalm 19:1-6 and Romans 1:20 give another.

3. Even though nature itself teaches us many things about our Creator, there are some things that it cannot teach. What other source must we use to learn about the Creator? List some things revealed in the Bible that are not revealed through nature.

4. There are many things in this Universe that even the smartest human beings do not understand. What does this fact say about the designer of the Universe? Use Job chapters 38-41 to help with the answer.

5. Brilliant inventors have designed camcorders and other technological wonders. What does that say for parts of the body such as the eye and the brain that are more advanced than any technology?

"Righteous are You, O Lord, when I plead with You; yet let me talk with You about Your judgments. Why does the way of the wicked prosper? Why are those happy who deal treacherously?"

Jeremiah 12:1

If there is an all-powerful God, and if He really is all-good, then why do bad things happen to innocent people?

EVIL, PAIN, AND SUFFERING

John sat on the end of his bed with his head buried deeply in his hands. His face was red, tear-stained, and puffy from several days of ceaseless crying. The past few days all seemed to run together, but he could remember quite well how it all started. Jennifer, his lovely girlfriend for the past three years, was sitting in the passenger seat talking about the movie they had just watched. Suddenly, the headlights in the other lane swerved in front of John's car. He slammed on the breaks and began to turn the steering wheel hard to the left. When he did, the oncoming car crashed into the passenger's side. John made it out of the wreck with only a few cuts and scratches, and so did the drunk who caused the accident, but Jennifer was rushed to the hospital. After several hours of surgery, a nervous-looking doctor walked into the small room where John was waiting. "Are you John Smith?" he asked. "Yes, I am" replied John. "How is she?" The doctor took him by the arm, looked him in the eye, and said: "I'm terribly sorry, but your girlfriend has died. We tried our best, but there was nothing more we could do."

Now, as John sat on his bed, two weeks after Jennifer's death, questions raged in his mind. Jennifer always had been very religious; she went to church twice on Sundays, and every Wednesday night for Bible study. She was heavily involved with the "meals on wheels" program, and even had talked John into going to Peru last year to take part in a door-knocking campaign. Why did God let her die? Why didn't the Lord take the drunk driver who had caused the accident, or the drug dealer on the other side of town? Why Jennifer? John just kept thinking, "If God is so kind and loving, and if He is all-powerful, then why does He allow innocent people to suffer and die?"

John came face-to-face with a problem that practically every person eventually encounters: If there is an all-powerful God, and if He is all-good, then why do bad things happen to innocent people? Many people have abandoned their belief in God because of the presence of suffering in their lives or in the lives of those close to them. Some have lost children, others have uttered what they feel are unanswered prayers, and still others have seen their very best friends tragically taken from them. Faced with these terrible events, they have decided that there is no God.

For example, in the 1960s, a very religious young man from Chattanooga, Tennessee was a shining example to his peers. He led a prayer group and even planned to do foreign mission work—until his sister died of leukemia and his father committed suicide. The boy's belief in God collapsed, and he became one of America's most outspoken unbelievers and pro-abortion advocates. The boy's name?—Ted Turner, founder of world-famous CNN, the Turner Broadcasting System, and other well-known media enterprises.

WHY DOES GOD ALLOW SUFFERING?

Let's begin to answer this question by making it clear that the Word of God must be used as the main source in this discussion; after all, both the problem and the solution can be found within its pages. Think with me. Where does the idea originate that God is all-powerful? It does not come from science or philosophy. Rather, the idea comes straight from passages within the Bible such as Genesis 17:1 where God said, "I am Almighty God," or Matthew 19:26 where Jesus said, "With men this is impossible, but with God all things are possible." And the same principle applies to the idea that God is all-loving (1 John 4:8,16).

Unfortunately, when we appeal to the Bible for an answer to the problem of evil, pain, and suffering, some people object. They say that we should not use the Bible, but they do not realize that **they** used the Bible to formulate the problem. After all, if the Bible did not teach that God is all-loving and all-powerful, then this problem would not exist in the first place. Therefore, we can and must use the Bible to find the solution to the problem.

After God had finished creating everything, it was very good (Genesis 1:31). However, Adam and Eve sinned against God, and as a result brought pain and suffering into the world. God always has given human beings the right to make their own decisions. He did not create us as robots that have no choice. In Psalm 32:9, King David wrote: "Do not be like the horse or like the mule, which have no understanding, which must be harnessed with bit and bridle, else they will not come near you." God never has forced (and never will force) humans to obey Him. He does not want us to be like the horse or mule that must be forced into His service. Instead, He graciously allows humans to make their own decisions. Much of the suffering present in the world today is a direct result of the misuse of the freedom of choice of past generations. Paul wrote in Romans 5:18: "Therefore, as through one man's offense judgment came to all men." Mankind—not God—is to blame for the suffering in this world.

But do not think that **all** the pain and suffering in this world can be blamed on past generations. Each one of us makes wrong decisions and incorrect judgments by which we bring pain upon ourselves and upon others. The young man who decides to "sow his wild oats" eventually will learn that every person reaps what he sows (Galatians 6:7).

Many destitute people have awakened in a gutter because they freely chose to get drunk the night before. Many teenage girls have become pregnant out of wedlock due to poor decisions and lack of will power. And many drunk drivers have killed themselves, their passengers, and innocent victims, because they would not relinquish the keys.

As young people, you must understand that all of your actions have consequences. What you do today determines what your life will be like tomorrow. God will allow you to be forgiven of your sins, but He will not always remove the painful consequences of your actions. Much of the pain and suffering that we experience in this world is our own fault.

In addition, God created a world ruled by natural laws. If a man steps off the roof of the Empire State Building, gravity will pull him to the pavement beneath. If a boy steps in front of a moving freight train, the momentum of the train most likely will kill the child. All of nature is regulated by natural laws set in place by God. They are the same for everyone (believer and unbeliever alike). In Luke 13:2-5, Jesus told the story of eighteen people who died when the tower of Siloam fell on them. Did they die because they were more wicked or more deserving of death than others around them? No, they died because of natural laws that were in effect. Fortunately, natural laws are constant so that we can study them and benefit from them. We are not left to sort out some kind of random system that works one day but not the next.

Furthermore, there are times when suffering is beneficial. Think of the man whose chest begins to throb as he begins to have a heart attack, or the woman whose side starts to ache at the onset of appendicitis. Pain often sends us to the doctor for prevention or cure. Also, tragedy can help humans develop some of the most treasured traits known to mankind—bravery, heroism, and self-sacrifice—all of which flourish in less-than-perfect circumstances. Yet those who exhibit such qualities are said to go "above and beyond the call of duty." Wasn't that the point Christ was making in John 15:13 when He said, "Greater love has no one than this, than to lay down one's life for his friends"?

But sometimes there seems to be no logical explanation for the immense suffering that a person is experiencing. Take the Old Testament character of Job as an example. He lost ten children and all of his wealth in a few short hours. Yet the Bible describes him as upright and righteous. Why would God allow such a man to suffer? James 1:2-3 helps us see the answer: "My brethren, count it all joy when you fall into various trials, knowing that the testing of your faith produces patience." Jesus Christ was the only truly innocent man ever to live, yet He suffered immensely. The fact is, pain and suffering have benefits that we sometimes cannot see. But God knows what will be better for us in the long run.

Instead of blaming God for pain or denying His existence, we should look to Him for strength and let tragedies remind us that this world never was intended to be our final home (read Hebrews 11:13-16). James 4:14 reminds us that our time on this Earth is extremely brief. The fact that even the Son of God was subjected to terrible evil, pain, and suffering (Hebrews 5:8; 1 Peter 2:21ff.) proves that God does love and care for His creation. He could have abandoned us to our own sinful devices, but instead "God demonstrates His own love toward us, in that while we were still sinners, Christ died for us" (Romans 5:8).

The current evil, pain, or suffering that an unbeliever endures is difficult to understand at times, but it is not the greatest tragedy of his life. The greatest tragedy of the unbeliever's life—for now and for eternity—is his unwillingness to see the love of God.

DISCUSSION QUESTIONS

1. In the first century, what was a major opinion concerning the cause of pain and death (John 9:1-3; Luke 13:1-5)? In what two ways did Jesus alter the popular opinion on the issue?

2. Jesus taught that a person's suffering is not always the result of his or her sinful behavior (John 9:1-3). Many righteous people suffer while, on the other hand, some very sinful people prosper. How, then, do we explain such biblical statements as those found in Proverbs 10:6 and 12:7. (Note that the entire book of Job deals with this issue.)

3. Discuss some instances in which pain can be beneficial. Use both physical and spiritual examples. James 1:1-5, 2 Corinthians 7:8-10, and Proverbs 13:24 can help.

4. Even though all suffering is not a result of individual sin, some is. Discuss ways that people bring suffering on themselves. How do Romans 1:27, Hebrews 12:4-11, and Proverbs 23:29-35 influence this discussion?

5. Think about the suffering that may have occurred in your life. What suffering did you bring upon yourself? What have you learned from it? How can you use what you have learned to help others?

"All Scripture is given by inspiration of God, and is profitable for doctrine, for reproof, for correction, for instruction in righteousness, that the man of God may be complete, thoroughly equipped for every good work."

2 Timothy 3:16-17

Inspiration guarantees that the writers of Holy Scripture would not make factual, historical, or scientific errors, since God as the author is all-knowing.

IS THE BIBLE FROM GOD?

— Part 1 —

Suppose you were talking on the telephone with one of your friends, and your six-year-old brother came into your room and demanded that you get off the phone. Most of the time, you simply would ignore him and continue your conversation. But suppose he were to barge in and demand that you immediately get off the phone by saying something like, "Mom said to" or "Dad told me to tell you to." His demand would carry more weight or authority the second time, because someone higher up than your little brother actually was making the request.

So it is with the Bible. If it cannot be proven that the Bible is the inspired Word of God, then it carries little more weight than the demand of a six-year-old sibling. But if the Bible is the Word of God, then **everything** it says must be obeyed because all the authority of the Creator stands behind it.

WHAT DOES "INSPIRED" MEAN?

Oftentimes we hear people talk about the "inspired" Word of God. But what does "inspired" really mean. The word inspire comes from the Latin word *inspirare*, which means "to breathe upon or into." If we say, then, that the Bible is inspired, we simply mean that God breathed His Word into the men who wrote it down. This would guarantee that the writers of Holy Scripture would not make factual, historical, or scientific errors, since God, as the Author, is omniscient (all-knowing).

It requires a considerable amount of evidence to show that the Bible is "God-breathed." First, we must establish that the Bible actually claims to be the inspired Word of God. Second, we must demonstrate that the Bible contains things that no other book written by mere men could contain.

DOES THE BIBLE CLAIM TO BE INSPIRED BY GOD?

If your little six-year-old brother never informed you that he was speaking for your parents, then you probably would not listen to him. In the same way, if the Bible never claimed to be the Word of God, then most people would not listen to, or obey, what it says.

However, numerous verses within the Bible present the claim that it is the Word of God. One of the best-known passages is 2 Timothy 3:16-17: "All Scripture is given by inspiration of God, and is profitable for doctrine, for reproof, for correction, for instruction in righteousness, that the man of God may be complete, thoroughly equipped for every good work." In this particular passage, the apostle Paul explained to the young preacher

Timothy that the Bible is the most valuable book ever known to man, due to the fact that it is God-breathed.

Another passage that documents the Bible's claim of inspiration is 2 Peter 1:20-21: "Knowing this first, that no prophecy of Scripture is of any private interpretation, for prophecy never came by the will of man, but holy men of God spoke as they were moved by the Holy Spirit."

In fact, over 2,700 times the Bible says something to the effect of "the Lord said" or this is "the Word of the Lord." That is truly amazing, considering that many Bibles have only about 1,200 pages. On average, the Bible claims that it is God's Word a little over two times per page.

Of course, just because the Bible **claims** to be the Word of God does not mean that it **is**. I can claim to be President of the United States, but that does not make me President. In order to prove that the Bible actually is inspired by God, we must show that it contains things that no other book in the world could contain.

AMAZING FACTS ABOUT THE BIBLE

First, the manner in which the Bible was written is nothing short of remarkable. It was written over a period of about 1,600 years by approximately 40 different writers who came from a variety of different backgrounds and educational levels. Some were lowly fishermen, some were humble farmers, some were well-educated scribes, and some were kings. Yet when we look at this book—written by such a diversity of men over so many years—it exhibits an amazing unity, as if a single, guiding hand was behind it.

The Old Testament starts with the beginning of the Universe and ends in Malachi with the promise of a coming Messiah. The New Testament starts with the birth of the Messiah in Matthew and ends in Revelation with the destruction of the Universe and the promise of heaven.

The unity of the Bible truly is remarkable, especially when compared to what we might expect from ordinary human authors. What if we took a banker from New York, a farmer from Missouri, and a preacher from Tennessee and asked them to write an essay on the history of the United States. Can you imagine how much they would disagree? And they would be writing at the same time! Yet, when we look at the Bible—written over a period of 1,600 years by about 40 different men—we see astounding agreement. The penman who recorded information about Jesus' death in Psalm 22:16-18 (1,000 years before it happened!) agreed perfectly with Matthew's account (27:35). Also, the concluding chapter of Malachi (the last book in the Old Testament) foretold the coming of "Elijah the prophet" and the first chapters of Mark, Luke, and John (three of the first four books in the New Testament) document the life of John the Baptist, who was the figurative Elijah discussed in Malachi (Matthew 17:1-13). From cover to cover, all the writers agree about the fall of mankind, the qualities of the Creator, and the glory of Christ the Messiah. No human author could have written the Bible.

Scientific Foreknowledge

The unity of the Bible is indeed remarkable, but there are many other areas that show the Bible to be beyond the capabilities of human authors. The Bible presents astonishing facts that the writers, on their own, simply could not have known.

In Genesis 6:15, God instructed Noah to build an ark that was 300 cubits long, 50 cubits wide, and 30 cubits high. This is a ratio of 30 to 5 to 3 (length to breadth to height). Until 1858, the ark was the largest floating ship on record. In terms that we understand better, the ark was about 450 feet long, 75 feet wide, and 45 feet high. In 1844, a man named Isambard K. Brunnel built his giant ship, the *Great Britain*. He used almost the exact ratio of the ark—30:5:3. As it turns out, these dimensions are the perfect ratio for a huge boat built for seaworthiness and not for speed. (Obviously the ark wasn't built for speed, since it had nowhere to go.) During World War II, shipbuilders employed a similar ratio to build a boat that eventually was nicknamed the "ugly duckling." It was a barge-like boat built to carry tremendous amounts of cargo. The United States Navy had years of experience upon which to draw when it came time to construct its ship. But how did Noah know the perfect seagoing ratio to use in building his ark? Brunnel and others like him had many generations of shipbuilding knowledge to use, but Noah's boat literally was the first of its kind. Where did he get such information? From the Master Builder!

Medical Practices of the Bible

Another area in which the Bible was way ahead of its time is the field of medicine. In Leviticus 17:11-14, Moses told the Israelites that "the life of the flesh is in the blood." He was absolutely right. In fact, human red blood cells carry about 270,000,000 molecules of hemoglobin per cell. It's a good thing they carry so much, because hemoglobin is the substance in the cell that carries oxygen. Without the necessary amount of hemoglobin and oxygen, a good hard sneeze or swift pat on the back could deplete a person of the oxygen needed to stay alive.

Today, we recognize the truthfulness of the statement that "the life of the flesh is in the blood." But we haven't known that for very long. For example, George Washington, the first President of the United States, was bled to death by his doctors. In the late 1700s and early 1800s, doctors often "bled" their patients. They thought that the blood contained evil "vapors," and that the only way to remove the vapors was to get rid of some of the blood. Today, of course, we know that is not true. Think of all the lives that have been saved by simple blood transfusions. Yes, today we know the truth of the matter. But how did Moses know it thousands of years ago? Just a lucky guess?

Another practice that Old Testament people could not have initiated on their own can be found in Deuteronomy 23:12-14 where Moses commanded the children of Israel to go outside the camp to bury human waste products. We now know that this is a sound public hygiene practice, but we haven't always known that. In Moses' day, and for thousands of years thereafter, numerous societies dumped human wastes in any convenient place. In Europe during the Middle ages, "Black Plague" [bubonic plague] swept over the continent on two different occasions, killing more than 13 million people. Why? The common European practice was to dump human wastes into the public streets. There, a germ known as *Yersinia pestis* grew in the waste. This germ contaminated the fleas that wallowed in the waste. The fleas then attached themselves to rats. The rats invaded people's houses and the fleas jumped onto humans, biting them and infecting them with the plague organism. Millions of lives were lost. If the people had obeyed God's simple commandment as given by Moses in Deuteronomy 23, all the pain and death of the epidemics could have been prevented. How did Moses know, thousands of years earlier, how to prevent such epidemics? Simple—he had a direct connection to the Great Physician.

CONCLUSION

The Bible makes the claim to be the inspired Word of God. In this lesson, we have looked at its amazing unity and its scientific foreknowledge. In the next chapter, we will examine the Bible's ability to predict the future. No other book in the world has outlasted the Bible. It provides information that no other book can equal. When the Bible speaks, we should pay close attention because "all scripture is given by inspiration of God."

DISCUSSION QUESTIONS

1. If a man demanded the keys to your car, why would it make a difference if he wore a badge or not? What relationship does power have to authority? In Matthew 21: 23, the Pharisees were treating Jesus like a "little brother" who had no authority to tell them what to do. How did Jesus prove that He had God's authority? How does the Bible prove it has God's authority?

2. List some verses other than the ones in the text that talk about the inspiration of the Bible. How would we react if God were talking directly to us, rather than speaking through the Scriptures? How would our reaction compare to that of the Israelites in Exodus 20:18-20? Would our attitude toward the reading of Scripture change?

3. Just because the Bible claims to be the Word of God does not make it so. We must provide evidence to prove its inspiration. How is that similar to the life of a Christian? What things can one use to "prove" his or her Christianity? Refer to John 13:35, James 1:27, 2:14-26, and 1 John 3:18.

4. Why can it be said with accuracy that the Bible exhibits amazing unity? What is the main theme of the Bible? Who are some of the main characters (mentioned in several books), and what do they have or not have in common?

5. What effect have scientific discoveries in the field of medicine had on the Bible? (By "discoveries," we mean actual documentation of some natural fact.) What will happen to the Bible as science makes new discoveries?

"When the word of the prophet comes to pass, the prophet will be known as one whom the Lord has truly sent."

Jeremiah 28:9

Time after time, the Bible has been "dead on" when it has predicted the future.

IS THE BIBLE FROM GOD?
— Part 2 —

PROPHECY

You have the remote control in your hand and a bag of potato chips resting securely between your leg and the armrest. It's 9:00 p.m. and you're channel surfing, trying to find a decent show to watch. Even though your particular cable system can pick up 150 channels, you can't seem to find anything that appeals to you.

But there's one thing that annoys you even more than the fact that you can't locate anything to watch. About every third channel, some lady pops up on the screen advertising the "Psychic Hotline." That's right, for "only" $1.95 a minute you can call and have someone tell you things that they think are going to happen in the future regarding your career, love life, popularity, etc. As cheesy as the advertising is, and as absurd as it sounds, people spend thousands of dollars every month calling to find out "what is going to happen in the future."

Truth be told, being able to predict the future accurately would be quite valuable. Imagine knowing who would win every Super Bowl for the next 20 years. If that kind of information fell into the hands of someone who gambled, he easily could become a millionaire by placing the right bets. But we know that no one today can tell the future without being wrong most of the time. Sure, some people make a lucky guess every now and then, but sooner or later their predictions fall through.

However, if someone could be 100% right 100% of the time, how important (and impressive!) would that be? The Bible provides the answer: "When the word of the prophet comes to pass, the prophet will be known as one whom the Lord has truly sent" (Jeremiah 28:9). If someone (or something, like a book) could predict the future and be correct 100% of the time, then obviously that ability came directly from God. So, the question arises, "Is there such a person or book?" Let's take a closer look and see.

The Fall of Tyre

In Ezekiel 26:1-14, the Bible foretells with miraculous precision the destruction of the ancient city of Tyre. The prophet Ezekiel predicted that Nebuchadnezzar, King of Babylon, would destroy the city (26:7-8). Many nations would come up against Tyre (26:3). The city would be leveled and scraped clean like a bare rock (26:4), and its stones, timbers, and soil would be cast into the sea (26:12). The surrounding area would become a spot for the spreading of fishermen's nets (26:5). And, last, the city never would be rebuilt to its former glory (26: 14).

To the people who heard Ezekiel, such predictions would have seemed unusual. In many instances, whenever a city was destroyed by an invading army, it was rebuilt using the same materials, since such materials were costly and hard to get.

Documented secular history records that each one of Ezekiel's predictions came true. Tyre was a coastal city that had a somewhat unusual arrangement. In addition to the inland city, there also was an island about three-fourth's of a mile offshore. Nebuchadnezzar besieged the mainland city in 586 B.C., but when he finally was able to take the city (in about 573 B.C.), his victory was hollow. He did not realize that the inhabitants had abandoned the city and moved to the island—a situation that remained virtually unchanged for the next 241 years. Then, in 332 B.C., Alexander the Great conquered the city—but not with ease. To get to the island, he literally had his army "scrape clean" the inland city of all timbers, stones, and dirt. He had his soldiers dump those materials into the ocean, thereby constructing a "land bridge" to the island city, which he conquered fairly quickly.

The prophet Ezekiel looked hundreds of years into the future and predicted that the original city of Tyre would never regain its position of wealth and power. Instead, it would be a bald rock where groups of fishermen would gather to spread their nets. And that is exactly what history records as having happened.

How could Ezekiel have known—without God having told him ahead of time—that all of these events would take place in history?

Babylon the Great

Another strikingly accurate prophecy concerning the ancient city of Babylon can be found in the Bible. Babylon was one of the richest cities in the world during the years 740 B.C. to 680 B.C. During those "glory days," the city prospered like it had the "Midas touch"; everything it touched seemed to turn to gold. It was located between the Tigris and the Euphrates rivers—a strip of land so agriculturally productive that today it is known as the "fertile crescent."

But its agriculture and well-watered plains were not the reason it was famous. Babylon gained its reputation because of its high, massive walls and its strong defensive battlements. In fact, ancient writers described walls that were 14 miles long on all four sides of the city and that reached heights of over 300 feet—taller than many buildings today. Not only were the walls long and high, but in some places they were 75-feet thick. The walls were not the only form of defense, however. The Euphrates River surrounded the city, providing a perfect moat that ranged anywhere from 65 to 250 feet across. This defensive combination appeared to make the city unconquerable.

Yet in spite of its strong military and defensive strength, God's prophets foretold Babylon's destruction. In Jeremiah 50:9, the prophet declared that God would "raise and cause to come up against Babylon an assembly of great nations from the north country." This prediction probably seemed unfounded at the time it was made, because none of the countries in the north came close to having enough strength to defeat Babylon. But years after the prophecy, Cyrus, king of the Medo-Persian Empire, mounted a huge force of many different nations and marched southward against Babylon.

The details of the fulfillment of the prophecy are nothing short of amazing. Jeremiah recorded that God had declared: "I will dry up her sea and make her springs dry" (51:36). Again the prophet foretold: "A drought is against her waters, and they will be dried up. For it is a land of carved images" (50:38). Also, the prophet promised that the Lord had spoken: "I will prepare their feasts; I will make them drunk, that they may rejoice, and sleep a perpetual sleep and not awake" (51:39).

Now listen to the story as history unfolds. The Euphrates River ran underneath the walls of Babylon. After a siege of two years, Cyrus finally was able to divert the river to make it flow into a huge marsh on the western side of the city. By doing this, he "dried up the rivers" of Babylon and provided an easy way for his soldiers to enter the city under the walls where water once flowed. But the Babylonians inside the city had no idea what was taking place. They could have defended the city, but instead they were feasting and getting drunk. Cyrus ordered his men to act like drunken revilers, and by the time the people of Babylon knew what had hit them, the city was filled with enemy troops who ultimately conquered it.

Even though these circumstances would be enough to establish the accuracy of the prophecy of Jeremiah (and thus of the Bible itself), the prophet's predictions do not stop there. Chapters 50-51 of Jeremiah's book are filled with more futuristic condemnations of Babylon, each of which was fulfilled in the smallest detail. Truly, the words spoken by the prophet came to pass.

The Coming Christ

In addition to its prophecies concerning people, places, and events, the Old Testament contains more than three hundred "messianic" prophecies. A messianic prophecy is one that tells about the coming "Messiah" or Savior. These prophecies were written to tell the world about the One Who would come to save humankind from sin. The prophecies concerning the Messiah said that He would be rejected and know grief (Isaiah 53:3), and be betrayed by a friend (Psalm 41:9) for thirty pieces of silver (Zechariah 11:12). In fact, He was rejected and betrayed (John 13:18; Matthew 26:15). He would be spit upon and beaten (Isaiah 50:6; 53:5), and in death His hands and feet were to be pierced (Psalm 22:16). This is exactly what happened (Matthew 27:30; Luke 24:39). Although He would die and be placed in a rich man's tomb (Isaiah 53:9; Matthew 27:57), His bones would not be broken (Psalm 34:20; John 19:33), nor would His flesh see corruption, because He would be raised from the dead (Psalm 16:10; Acts 2:22ff.) and eventually ascend into heaven (Psalm 110:1-3; 45:6; Acts 1:9-10). These prophecies were written hundreds of years before they were fulfilled. But Jesus Christ fulfilled each of them in every detail. Although the stories of men's lives generally are written **after** they die, the history of Christ's life was written **before He was even born**! How? Because God inspired the prophets who wrote the accounts. No book but the Bible contains such prophetic accuracy.

CONCLUSION

Time after time, the Bible has been "dead on" when it has predicted the future. Secular records document the facts about Tyre, Babylon, and even Jesus Christ. So what does all this prove? It proves one simple thing —that God Himself inspired the words written between the covers of the Bible. And because that is the case, every human being should welcome the Bible "not as the word of men, but as it is in truth, the word of God" (1 Thessalonians 2:13).

DISCUSSION QUESTIONS

1. Many people are willing to make "predictions." Discuss the differences, however, between an "educated guess" and true prophecy.

2. What is conditional prophecy? Explain why prophecies like 2 Kings 20:1 and Jonah 3:4 were not fulfilled. Do such "unfulfilled" prophecies hurt the Bible's credibility? Why or why not?

3. People always have wanted to know the future. In ancient times, many resorted to astrology and sorcery in hopes of predicting the future (2 Chronicles 33:6). Why is knowing the future so important to some people? Which kind of test is easier to take—one for which you know the exact questions beforehand, or one for which you must study all your notes?

4. Much of the prophecy in the Bible was written to alter certain people's behavior (see 2 Kings 20:1 and Jonah 3:4). What is the single most important future event about which God has informed humans, and how should knowledge of it alter human behavior (2 Peter 3:10-13)?

5. God has proven that He knows the future. Is there a difference between **knowing** everything that will happen in the future and **causing** everything to happen? How does freedom of choice fit into this discussion? Factor into your answer 1 Timothy 2:3-4 and Matthew 7:13-14.

"The entirety of Your word is truth, and every one of Your righteous judgments endures forever."

Psalm 119:160

After the Bible has been put under the high-powered microscope of criticism, and dissected by the razor-sharp scalpel of supposed contradictions, it rises from the surgery with no scratches or scars, none the worse for wear.

ARE THERE MISTAKES
IN THE BIBLE?

The light shone brightly into the eyes of the suspect, who was seated between two FBI agents in black suits. "Where were you the night of October 31?," demanded one of the agents. The suspect nervously muttered, "I already told you, I was at a Halloween party with some friends." The interrogation continued: "And what, exactly, were you doing at the party?" asked the same demanding voice. "I bobbed for apples," retorted the suspect in his shaky voice. Several hours later, during another interrogation, a different FBI agent asked the suspect what seemed to be a silly question: "Have you ever bobbed for apples?" The suspect promptly replied, "No, never in my life have I bobbed for apples."

Obviously, the suspect was lying. He could not say truthfully with one breath that he bobbed for apples, and then in the next breath say that he never in all his life had bobbed for apples. Either he had or he had not bobbed for apples; both statements could not be true.

Some people accuse the Bible of doing the exact same thing as the lying suspect. They claim that when the Bible is put under close scrutiny it says one thing in one place, and then says something totally contradictory in another.

If the Bible does contradict itself, then the Christian has some serious problems. The Christian claims that the Bible is the Word of God. Yet if it contradicts itself, then that would make God a liar. And since the Bible states that God cannot lie (Titus 1:2), then any book with contradictions in it could not have been inspired by God. Therefore, if legitimate contradictions can be found anywhere in the Bible, then it is not the inspired Word of God.

Skeptics claim to have found not just one, but hundreds of contradictions. And the sincere Bible reader will admit that occasionally even he comes across something in a passage that seems to "contradict" something else in the Bible.

ARE BIBLE "CONTRADICTIONS" REAL?

Let it be noted that if the Bible does, in fact, contain a legitimate contradiction of some kind, it has not yet been found. When all the facts are considered, each alleged biblical contradiction has been documented to be something other than a true contradiction. That is a powerful statement, considering the fact that no book in the world has been examined more closely or scrutinized more carefully. After the Bible has been put under the high-powered microscope of criticism, and dissected by the razor-sharp scalpel of supposed contradictions, it rises from the surgery with no scratches or scars, none the worse for wear.

A Copy of a Copy

When we say that the Bible contains no contradictions, we must be clear about the fact that we are discussing the Bible as it existed in its original form. When writers such as Matthew, Mark, Luke, John, Peter, and Paul penned their books, the finished product was completely without error or contradiction. However, over the many years from then to now, those books have been copied and reproduced thousands of times—many times by hand. Every time the Bible is recopied or translated into other languages, there is a slight chance that the uninspired humans doing the copying or translating will "mess up."

For example, in Acts 2:27, the King James Version indicates that Jesus' soul would go to hell, but would not be left there. Mark 9:43 describes hell as a place where **sinful** souls go to be punished for eternity. But the Bible says that Jesus was perfect, not sinful (1 Peter 1:19). Is this, then, an example of a contradiction? No, not at all. The problem here is that the translators of the King James Version should have placed the word "hades" in Acts 2:27, since hades is the realm of the dead where every soul goes after it leaves its earthly body. It is composed of two compartments—paradise and torment, as described in Luke 16:19-31. Jesus' soul never went to the lake of fire that burns forever (what the Bible refers to as "hell"). Rather, His soul went to the realm known as hades, where all souls—both righteous and unrighteous—go for a while. It was the translators of the King James Version who made the mistake, not the inspired author of Acts.

But do not be alarmed at the few mistakes that copiers and translators have made while reproducing the Bible. We have over 99% of the original text of the Bible, and **not one** of the questionable segments deals with a single article of faith. Most of the so-called "discrepancies" deal with questions like whether there should be an "a" instead of a "the" in a certain place, or whether a particular verse should say "the Lord" or "the Lord Jesus."

Just a Possibility

When dealing with so called contradictions, sometimes many different solutions will present themselves. In order to "fix" the contradiction, we do not necessarily have to nail down the **exact** solution. All that the biblical defender must do is offer a **possible** solution.

For instance, in Acts 7:16 the Bible says that Abraham bought a tomb in Shechem where the patriarchs were buried. However, in Joshua 24:32 the Bible plainly says that Jacob was the one who bought the plot of ground in Shechem where Joseph eventually was buried. At first glance then, it looks like a contradiction exists; but upon closer inspection, several possible solutions present themselves.

First, both men could have purchased the field. Jacob was in the area more than 150 years after Abraham. Abraham could have bought the field, sold it back, and Jacob could have bought the field many years later. The United States has been in existence only a little over 200 years. Imagine your great grandfather buying a field before the Civil War. In order for you to gain possession of the field today, you might have to buy it. Second, it is possible that Abraham bought a **tomb** in Shechem, but that Jacob bought a **field**. The Bible does not say that Jacob bought a tomb, but only a field (Genesis 33:19; Joshua 24:32).

The bottom line is that no one knows for sure exactly what happened with the field, the tomb, Abraham, or Jacob. But in order to avoid a contradiction, we simply must show that there is a **possibility** that the two statements could be true—which is exactly what we have done.

Just Answer the Questions, Please

Generally, most alleged contradictions can be solved by answering three simple questions: (1) Is the same person or thing under consideration?, (2) Is the same time period being discussed?, and (3) Is the same sense under consideration?

Think with me. Suppose that someone says, "Leroy Jones is rich," and "Leroy Jones is poor." Do those two statements automatically contradict each other? Not necessarily. Many people are named Leroy Jones (O.K., maybe not all that many, but at least two). It could be that Leroy Jones in Florida is rich, but Leroy Jones in New York is poor. The same person or thing must be under consideration.

Further, the same time period must be under consideration. Leroy Jones could have made a fortune in his early twenties as an oil tycoon and become very rich, but after a terrible stock market crash could have lost everything he owned. At one time, then, he was rich, but now, he is poor. The two statements could have been describing his life quite accurately at the time each was made.

Also, the statements must be talking about the same sense. Leroy Jones could have more money than anyone else in the entire world, but if he is not following God, then he is poor. On the other hand, he could have absolutely no money, but be rich in spiritual blessings. After all, "Has God not chosen the poor of this world to be rich in faith" (James 2:5)? Answering these three questions helps tremendously in resolving the contradiction controversy.

Supplementary, My Dear Watson

Another important principle that will help the honest reader wipe the grime off the window pane of alleged contradictions is that of **supplementation**. Suppose you are relating a story about the time you and some of your friends went shopping at the mall. You mention all the places in the mall to buy cinnamon rolls and play arcade games, and your friends tell about the great clothing stores. Is there a contradiction just because they mentioned clothing stores, while you mentioned only cinnamon rolls and arcade games? No. They simply are adding to (or supplementing) your story to make it more complete. That happens in the Bible as well (quite often, in fact).

As an example, in Matthew 14:21 the Bible says that Jesus fed about five thousand men, and that He also fed women and children. But in Mark 6:44, it says that He fed about five thousand men. Mark never mentions the women and children. Is that a contradiction? No, of course not. Did He feed about 5,000 men? Yes, and that makes Mark correct. Did Jesus break the loaves for about 5,000 men, along with some women and children?

Yes, which makes Matthew right, too. Just because one account "adds" some things does not mean that the accounts contradict each other.

Again, Matthew 27:57-60 says that Joseph of Arimathea took Jesus' body and placed it in his own tomb, but John 19:38-40 says that Joseph **and** Nicodemus placed the body in the tomb. Do they contradict each other? Certainly not! If one text said **only** Joseph did it, or **only** Nicodemus did it, then a contradiction might exist. But as it stands, John simply "adds" some facts to the account, just like your friends added some facts to your story about the mall. Supplementary accounts are not contradictory.

Casual Conversation

Suppose that the weatherman comes on the television and announces, "The Sun will rise at 6:03 a.m. on Saturday." Even though every one of us knows that the Earth rotates and the Sun really is not "rising" at all, we have no problem understanding the weatherman's comment. We call this "phenomenal" language—language that is used in everyday speech to refer to ordinary phenomena.

On occasion, the Bible likewise uses phenomenal language. For example, in Psalm 50:1, the writer describes the Sun as rising, and in 1 Corinthians 15:6 the apostle Paul spoke of some Christians who had died as having "fallen asleep." No one would accuse the weatherman of making a mistake when he suggests that the Sun will rise or set. In a similar fashion, the Bible writers should not be accused of making mistakes when they employ the same type of language.

CONCLUSION

Many unbelievers would like to discover just one real contradiction in the Bible. They have tried every way possible to twist and turn the Scriptures to force them to disagree. So far, they have been as unsuccessful as a man trying to cut a solid metal bar in half with a plastic butter knife. The future of such enterprises looks just as bleak. Along the way, many sincere Bible readers have stumbled across things that seem, at first glance, to be contradictory. Proper study and careful consideration on their part, however, have eliminated any hint of legitimate contradiction. Let the words of the psalmist be proclaimed: "Consider how I love Your precepts; Revive me, O Lord, according to Your lovingkindness. The **entirety** of Your word is **truth**, And every one of Your righteous judgments endures forever" (Psalm 119:159-160).

DISCUSSION QUESTIONS

1. Explain why the discussion of alleged biblical contradictions is so important. Why do some people **want** to find contradictions in the Bible?

2. Using the principles discussed in this chapter, explain how in Acts 12 James was killed with the sword, while in Acts 15 James was a leader in the Jerusalem church. Also, explain how Genesis 1:31 and Genesis 6:6 can be reconciled. Which principles did you use?

3. Discuss how John the Baptist could be "Elijah" and not be "Elijah" at the same time (Matthew 11:14; John 1:21). Explain how Paul could be "blameless," yet still be the "chief" of sinners (Philippians 3:6; 1 Timothy 1:15). Also, reconcile John 6:27 with 2 Thessalonians 3:10. Which principles from this chapter did you use to reconcile these verses?

4. What does "supplementary" mean? How does Luke 23:39-43 supplement Matthew 27:44? How does Matthew 20:29-34 supplement Mark 10:46-52?

5. Phenomenal language is just one example of the variety God put in the Bible. What is sarcasm? How is it used in James 2:19 and 2 Corinthians 12:13? How might phenomenal language and sarcasm in the Bible confuse some people?

"In the beginning God created the heavens and the earth."

Genesis 1:1

Facts are stubborn, impartial things that refuse to budge for people of high estate or low degree. The concepts of creation and evolution stand on opposite sides, and the facts stand behind only one of them. Which is it?

CREATION VERSUS EVOLUTION

To say that people sometimes disagree about the origin of the Universe would be a mild understatement. People not only disagree about how the Cosmos was formed, but even take each other to court over the matter! In fact, many public schools in the United States have been involved in some type of lawsuit between people who want the theory of evolution taught in the school system and those who want the concept of creation to have equal time. With so much controversy surrounding the issue of origins, we need to answer some important questions.

WHAT IS EVOLUTION?

Evolution is a scientific theory which claims that the Universe is **self-contained**, and that everything in the Universe has come into being through random processes over long periods of time without any outside cause (such as a Creator). According to evolution, no supernatural being had any part in the origin or development of life. Evolution claims that all living things originated from an original organism composed of only one cell, which in turn had arisen from something nonliving. Evolution states that all things originate through natural processes, and that nothing outside of nature exists.

WHAT IS CREATION?

Creation and evolution are exact opposites. According to creation, the Universe is **not self-contained**. A supernatural being—God—is responsible for the origin and design of the Universe. God used processes that are not still in operation today to carefully construct all things, including the various forms of life such as plants, animals, and humans.

WHICH VIEW IS RIGHT?

If you have paid close attention to the definitions of creation and evolution, you realize that they cannot both be correct. There is no room in evolution for a supernatural being such as God, and creation has no room for a purely natural process in which a single-celled organism eventually turns into humankind. The two theories are at odds, opposite, opposed, and contradictory. Therefore, only one of them can be correct. But which one is it?

Those of you reading this book might find it somewhat insulting to your intelligence if I simply told you which view is correct, but did not offer any evidence to support my conclusion. But since the factual evidence that is available points toward one of these two views, then a direct look at the facts should lead to the proper conclusion.

The Law of Biogenesis

In biology, one of the most widely respected laws of science is the Law of Biogenesis. "Biogenesis" is composed of two words—"bio," which means life, and "genesis," which means beginning. Thus, as you might suspect, this law deals with the beginning of life. And it simply says that life comes only from previous life of its own kind. We see this law play out everyday all around the world. Everyone knows that kittens come only from female cats, cows produce only calves, and puppies come only from dogs. A pig never gives birth to a horse, and a sheep never bears an iguana.

Over the years, the truthfulness of this law has been documented by thousands of scientists, one of the most famous of which was French microbiologist Louis Pasteur. His work dealt a crushing blow to the notion of spontaneous generation (the idea that life arises on its own from nonliving sources). In earlier centuries, the idea that life arose from nonliving things was very popular. People actually believed that a person could take some wheat grains, wrap them in an old rag, stuff them in the corner of a barn, and produce mice. They also believed that meat left on a kitchen counter would spontaneously generate maggots. However, teachers and professors today often point out (correctly!) how Pasteur triumphed over this "mythology" when he disproved the concept of spontaneous generation through his well-designed scientific experiments. Yet with almost their next breath, those same teachers and professors tell their students that evolution has occurred as a result of spontaneous generation.

The truth of the matter is that evolution could not have occurred without some form of spontaneous generation. For this reason, some scientists have concocted experiments in an attempt to create life from nonliving substances. But after all these attempts, life never has been created from something nonliving. Now, think critically for a moment. If scientists have **designed** carefully planned experiments to create life from something nonliving, and yet have failed miserably every time, how can we be expected to believe that "nature" did it using accidents, chance, and blind forces? On the contrary, whether **in nature or in the laboratory, scientists never have documented a single case of spontaneous generation**. Life comes only from previous life of its own kind, which is exactly what the creation model teaches.

What Do the Fossils Say?

Fossils are the remains of once-living organisms such as plants, animals, or humans that now are buried in the rocks of the Earth. They are found literally all over the globe, and help provide valuable information about life of the past. If any **physical** evidence exists to establish evolution, it certainly would have to come from the fossil record. But does it?

In order to establish evolution as true, its supporters must be able to document that the fossil record: (a) reveals a "chain" of organisms from simple to complex; and (b) contains transitional forms of plants and animals (and humans, for that matter). A transitional form is an organism that exhibits characteristics of two separate groups, such as a half reptile/half mammal.

Even Charles Darwin, who often is referred to as the "father of evolution," claimed that the fossil record must show "innumerable transitional links." In fact, he titled the tenth chapter of his book, *The Origin of Species,* "On the Imperfection of the Geological Record." Darwin suggested that "the number of intermediate varieties, which have formerly existed [must] be truly enormous." However, he admitted: "Geology assuredly does not reveal any such finely graduated chain; and this, perhaps, is the most obvious and serious objection which can be argued against this theory. The explanation lies, I believe, in the extreme imperfection of the geological record."

Darwin thought that further geological finds would document millions of transitional forms. But almost a hundred and forty-five years have passed since Darwin's day, and millions of additional fossils have been discovered. Yet the ever-elusive transitional forms still are missing. On occasion, scientists have produced **alleged** transitional forms (such as "Piltdown Man" or *Archaeopteryx*), but these are few and far between. Furthermore, on occasion some of them turn out to be frauds, and not one of them ever has been proven to be an authentic transitional form. The fact of the matter is, the fossil record still lacks the multitude of transitional forms predicted by Darwin and his followers—and will continue to do so. Why? **Because there are no transitional forms!**

Well, what **does** the fossil record show? It shows millions of organisms suddenly arriving on the scene fully formed and functional, without any transitional forms serving as their ancestors. Which of the two models of origins—creation or evolution—accounts for the sudden appearance of fully functional living organisms?

Things That Look Alike Must Be Related?

Sometimes you might see a person with an identical twin brother or sister. It is easy to tell that they are related because they look so much alike. Fathers and sons often look alike, as do mothers and daughters (or even some cousins). Many times, things that look similar are related to each other. Two black rabbits often have baby black rabbits, and two short dogs often produce offspring that are similarly short.

Undoubtedly, the idea that similarity frequently implies close relationship is one of the most impressive arguments for the theory of evolution. As scientists have worked in various fields, they have learned that certain similarities can be documented. If scientists observe **similarities in structure**, they refer to such structures as **homologous**. If, on the other hand, scientists observe **similarities in function**, they refer to such similarities as being **analogous**. For example, the wing of the bat, the forefoot of the turtle, the forefoot of the frog, and the arm of the man all have the same general structure. The forefoot of the dog, the flipper of the whale, and the hand of man contain essentially the same muscles and bones. Such organs thus are referred to as "homologous." Upon seeing this type of evidence, evolutionists conclude that all these creatures must be related because of their similarities.

How do creationists respond to such an argument? Well, they certainly do not deny the fact that similarities **do** exist. It is here, however that a valuable lesson can be learned in the creation/evolution controversy. That lesson is this: it rarely is the **facts** that are in dispute—it is the **interpretation** placed on the facts that is in dispute. When the creationist looks at the similarities that exist in nature, instead of claiming **common ancestry** he suggests that the evidence points to a **common designer**. For example, numerous GMC automobiles have wheels, body shapes, and brake systems similar to vehicles from the Ford Motor Company. Why so? Because they were designed for the same mode of travel. When the Creator designed a lung, brain, or nervous system that worked well, wouldn't it make sense that He would use these same essential features (with possible modification) in different organisms that were intended to live in the same environment, breathe the same air, and eat the same types of organic food? Similarity doesn't always show common ancestry; many times (in fact, more often than not) it shows common design.

Furthermore, when you consider **all** the similarities, they do not provide evidence of common ancestry. For example, the octopus eye, pig heart, Pekingese dog's face, and donkey's milk all have some structures similar to ones in the human body, but even evolutionists would deny that the animals in which they are found are closely related to each other or to humans.

CONCLUSION

The list of arguments used to support both evolution and creation could go on and on. There probably are as many arguments for each model of origins as there are scientists to make them. But we always must remember that the facts behind the arguments are the important things, not the false interpretation(s) of those facts.

The facts say that life comes only from previously existing life: evolution says life comes from nonliving sources. The facts show that no transitional forms of half-and-half organisms exist in the fossil record; evolution maintains that there should be millions of transitional forms. The facts show that similarities sometimes show common ancestry, but also can show common design. Facts are stubborn, impartial things that refuse to budge for people of high estate or low degree. The concepts of creation and evolution stand on opposite sides, and the facts stand behind only one of them. Which is it?

DISCUSSION QUESTIONS

1. What are several differences between creation and evolution? Why do many people clash over which one should be taught to children?

2. Dr. Louis Pasteur did experiments to disprove what false theory? Can you see why people might have held to that theory? How does that theory relate to evolution?

3. In order for evolution to be established, what must be found in the fossil record? What would you expect to find in the fossil record if creation is true? What do scientists actually find in the fossil record?

4. Similarities can show two things. What are they? How does the creationist answer the idea that similarities show common ancestry? What should creationists not do when answering such arguments?

5. Why does it matter what you believe about creation and evolution? Why do you think some people prefer to believe in evolution?

"This is the history of the heavens and the earth when they were created, in the day that the Lord God made the earth and the heavens."

Genesis 2:4

There are over seventy-five differ-ent scientific methods for calculating the age of the Earth, and most of them yield a relatively young age for our planet.

HOW OLD IS THE EARTH?

It is very difficult to find any common ground between creationists and evolutionists. In fact, the two groups disagree on just about every subject imaginable. But there is one area where they both see eye-to-eye—the age of the Earth. No, of course they do not agree about how old the Earth is, but they do concur that if the Earth is young (with an age measured in thousands of years instead of billions), then evolution never could have happened.

Therefore, evolutionists use every means at their disposal to "prove" that the Earth is very, very old. It is interesting to note that in Darwin's day, the Earth was considered to be only around 20 **million** years old, while today the Earth is alleged to be approximately 5 **billion** years old—or more than 250 times as old as it was during Darwin's day!

TRUE SCIENCE AND THE AGE OF THE EARTH

Even though most textbooks and science journals teach that the Earth is billions of years old, many scientific findings do not agree with such a concept (and, more important, the Bible does not agree—a point we will discuss later in this chapter). In fact, there are over seventy-five different scientific methods for calculating the age of the Earth, and most of them yield a relatively young age for our planet.

Fighting the Crowd

One of the strongest arguments for a young Earth comes from the field of human population statistics. According to historical records, the human population on Earth doubles approximately every 35 years. If you break down that figure, it represents an annual increase of 20,000 people per every million.[*] Let's suppose that humankind started with just two individuals (we will call them Adam and Eve for the sake of our argument). And suppose that they lived on the Earth 1 million years ago (some evolutionists suggest that man, in one form or another, has been on the Earth 3-5 million years). Suppose, further, that an average generation (the time a person lives) consisted of only 42 years, and that each family had an average of just 2.4 children. (They probably had many more than that, but we will use a conservative estimate that would allow for at least **some** population growth; if a family unit had only two children, there would be zero population growth, since each parent simply would replace himself or herself, providing no net increase.)

---

[*] Morris, Henry M. and John D. Morris (1996), *Creation Trilogy* (Green Forest, AR: Master Books), volume two, pp. 317-320.

Allowing for wars, famine, disease, etc., there would be approximately $1 \times 10^{5,000}$ people on the Earth today! That number is a 1 followed by 5,000 zeros. But the entire **Universe** (at an estimated size of 20 billion light-years in diameter) would hold only 1×10^{100} people. However, using creationist figures (of eight people having survived the Noahic Flood), the current world population would be in the general neighborhood of 4.34 billion people. Evolutionary figures thus would imply an Earth population $10^{4,900}$ times greater than would fit into the entire Universe! The question is, which of the two figures is almost right on target, and which could not possibly be correct?

To Decay or Not to Decay

To the "man on the street," one of the most impressive arguments for an ancient Earth is the testimony of sedimentary-rock layers. Scientists (and park rangers) show us examples like the Grand Canyon and present their theory so effectively that—as we observe layer after layer of sedimentary rocks piled one on top of another—the only explanation seems to be that vast eons of geologic time must have been involved. Each division of the rocks, we are told, represents a time long ago, and an ancient world that long since has ceased to exist. Creationists, however, beg to differ, and suggest that a closer look at the "record of the rocks" suggests youth, not antiquity, for our home planet.

Embedded in sedimentary rocks all over the globe are what are known as "polystrate" fossils. Polystrate simply means "many layers," and refers to fossils that cut through at least two sedimentary-rock layers. Probably the most widely recognized of the polystrate fossils are tree trunks that extend vertically through two, three, or more sections of rock that supposedly were laid down in epochs covering millions of years. However, organic material (such as wood) that is exposed to the elements will rot, not fossilize. Thus, the entire length of these tree trunks must have been preserved quickly, which suggests that the rock layers surrounding them must have been deposited rapidly (likely during a single catastrophe such as Noah's Flood).

The trees, reeds, catfish, whales, and other organisms with which the fossil record abounds did not die and then lie around for hundreds, thousands, or millions of years while slowly being turned into polystrate fossils. Truth be told, polystrate fossils testify loudly of a young Earth whose layers formed rapidly—not very long ago!

WHAT DOES THE BIBLE SAY?

The atheist, agnostic, or skeptic will find little of interest discussed under the above title. However, to the sincere student of God's Word, what the Bible says about the age of the Earth deserves serious consideration. For those who believe that there is a God, that Jesus is His Son, and that the Bible is His Word, this section offers the answer to the question of the Earth's age.

It certainly would have solved many problems if God had put a verse in the Bible that said something like: "When Jesus was born, the Earth was exactly 4,134 years old." But, no such statement can be found in the sacred text. That does not mean, however, that the biblical record does not contain information about the age of the Earth. Many times, in order to find out what the Bible says about a particular subject, we must look at many different verses and piece them together somewhat like a puzzle—which is precisely the case here. Therefore, let's examine one piece at a time.

In at least one sense, the Bible tells us exactly how old the Earth is. Moses wrote in Exodus 20:11: "For in six days, the Lord made the heavens and the **earth**, the sea, and all that is in them, and rested on the seventh day." In Mark 10:6, Jesus stated that "**from the beginning of the creation**, God made them male and female." The text in Genesis 1:26-31 explains that during that "beginning," God made mankind on day six of His creative activity. Since we know that the Earth was created on day one, and that man and woman were created on day six, that tells us that **the Earth is five days older than humanity!**

Thus, in order to calculate the age of the Earth, we must determine how long man has been here—a task that is not as difficult as it may seem at first glance. Speaking in round figures, how long has it been since Jesus Christ visited the Earth? The answer: about 2,000 years. Secular history volunteers that piece of information, since we are only a few years removed from A.D. 2000 (A.D. standing for *anno Domini*, meaning "in the year of the Lord"). Next, we must determine how many years passed between Jesus Christ and Abraham. Secular history also provides this information—which turns out to be around 2,000 years. These two figures can be obtained from practically any secular history book.

The final number we must uncover is the number of years between Abraham and Adam. Once we know this figure, simple addition of the three will give us the approximate age of the Earth. The figure representing the time between Abraham and Adam cannot be retrieved from secular history, nor should we expect it to be since the Flood would have destroyed most, if not all, of the records pertaining to that time period.

We have established the fact that Jesus was on the Earth about 2,000 years ago. In Luke 3, the writer lists 55 generations between Jesus and Abraham—a time that archaeology has determined to be around 2,000 years.[*] In that same chapter, Luke also documents that there were only 20 generations between Abraham and Adam. How much time passed during those twenty generations? Since Genesis 5 and 11 provide the ages of the fathers at the time of the births of their sons (between Abraham and Adam), it is a simple matter to calculate the approximate number of years—which turns out to be about 2,000. In chart form it looks like this:

1. Present time to Jesus	2,000 years
2. Jesus to Abraham	2,000 years (55 generations)
3. Abraham to Adam	2,000 years (20 generations)

The fact that the 55 generations between Jesus and Abraham cover 2,000 years, while only 20 generations between Abraham and Adam are required to cover the same amount of time, can be explained quite easily if we take into account the vast ages to which many of the patriarchs lived (Methuselah, for example, who lived 969 years, or Adam, who lived 930 years).

---

[*] Kitchen, Kenneth A. and J.D. Douglas, eds. (1982), *The New Bible Dictionary* (Wheaton, IL: Tyndale), second edition.

Some people have argued that the genealogies in Genesis 5 cannot be used to show the age of the Earth because they have huge "gaps" in them. But in Jude verse 14, the writer stated by inspiration that "Enoch was the **seventh** from Adam," (he is, in fact, listed exactly seventh in the genealogy found in Genesis 5:21). Therefore, we know that there are no gaps between the first seven patriarchs, because Jude confirmed the Old Testament statement. That leaves only 13 generations with any possible gaps between them. But in order to accommodate the evolutionary scenario (which suggests that man has been on the Earth in some form approximately 3.5 million years), it would be necessary to insert over 290,000 years between **each** of the 13 generations. And what would such "mathematical gymnastics" accomplish? Such an exercise would push the age of the Earth back to only 3.5 **million** years; evolutionists claim its age is in the neighborhood of 5 **billion** years! It does not require a wealth of either common sense or Bible knowledge to see that this quickly becomes ludicrous. Who could believe that the first seven of these generations are so exact, while the remaining 13 contain "gaps" of over 290,000 years each?

The Bible plainly teaches, after all the pieces of information have been put together, that the Earth is only about 6,000 years old.

APPARENT AGE

"But the Earth **looks** so old," some people will say. There are at least two responses to such a statement. First, one might ask: "Compared to what; what does a **young** Earth look like?" We do not have another Earth with which to compare this one, so just how would we know what a "young" Earth is supposed to look like? Second, it should not surprise us if science occasionally calculates older dates for the Earth, due to a scriptural concept known as the "doctrine of apparent age."

This idea suggests that the things God made during the Creation week were formed complete and fully functional. For instance, how old were Adam and Eve two seconds after God created them? They were two seconds old! Yet they walked, talked, and looked like adult human beings, and even had the ability to reproduce (which was one of the commands God gave them—Genesis 1: 28). If a tree were cut down in the Garden of Eden one day after the Creation week, how many rings would it have had? Possibly hundreds, yet it would have been only five days old (trees and other plants, remember, were created on day three of the Creation week). So, the **real** age of the tree and the **apparent** age of the tree would have been many years apart. Just because this Earth may **appear** older than 6,000 years, that does not mean it **is** older than that.

However, we must be careful not to "read into" the Bible things that are not there. For example, some people have asked if the doctrine of apparent age means that God placed plants and animals in the fossil record to "trick" man or "test his faith"? No, God never would do that. Why? When we find a fossil, we naturally (and correctly) believe that the organism that made the fossil once lived on Earth. **If** God just "inserted" it into the fossil record, then He has misled us or lied to us. Yet the Bible plainly teaches us that God cannot lie (Titus 1:2). How, then, did the vast numbers of plants and animals (and, occasionally, humans) become entombed in the fossil record? Likely, many of the fossils we see are the result of the Flood of Noah.

Other people have suggested that if God made the Earth appear older than it actually is, then He has deceived us because things aren't really as old as they might look. This criticism would be true—except for one thing: **God told us what He did!** He did not leave us in the dark, or try to "trick us" or "test our faith," by hiding from us important information that we would need. Rather, He was very straightforward and honest with us. Considering the material found in the first eleven chapters of Genesis (and elsewhere through the Bible), no one can justifiably accuse God of deception. If we ignore His Word regarding what He said He did, is it God's fault? Hardly!

CONCLUSION

The age of the Earth continues to be one of the most controversial topics between creationists and evolutionists. Although evolutionists certainly agree that a young Earth would disprove evolution, they most definitely do not agree that the Earth is young. However, many scientific data (such as population statistics, polystrate fossils, and numerous others) establish the fact that the Earth cannot be billions of years old. More important, the Bible teaches us that the Earth is only about 6,000 years old. In truth, the Earth and the rest of the Universe are only five days older than mankind. The birthday cake of the Universe has room for only about 6,000 candles, and evolutionists certainly can't blow out the evidence for that fact with a single breath.

DISCUSSION QUESTIONS

1. Use the genealogies provided in Genesis 5 to calculate how many years there were between Adam and the Flood. Then discuss what happened to mankind in that short period of time.

2. Discuss the doctrine of apparent age. How might that idea distort many scientific findings and modern dating methods?

3. Human population statistics and polystrate fossils are legitimate scientific methods which suggest that the Earth is relatively young. Why do you think that this type of information is not in the average public school science textbook? Is it any less scientific than the other information that is included in such books?

4. Why are archaeology and secular history valuable tools when talking to a skeptic? How can they help determine the age of the Earth? What are some of the limitations of these tools that do not apply to the Bible?

5. The verses in the Bible that provide information about the Earth's age must be "pieced together" from several places within the text. List several good reasons that might explain why God arranged it this way. Fit into your answer verses such as Matthew 7:7-11 and 2 Timothy 2:15.

"You shall not add to the word which I command you, nor take from it, that you may keep the commandments of the Lord your God which I command you."

Deuteronomy 4:2

A person cannot logically believe that the Bible is true, and then at the same time believe that evolution is true.

DOES THE BIBLE LEAVE ROOM FOR EVOLUTION?

It is very unpopular in the field of science to believe that God created the world in six literal, 24-hour days. In fact, according to most scientists, the Universe took billions of years to form, and thus it would be absurd to believe that it was created in just six days. Because of the prevailing idea of an ancient Cosmos, many people have tried to find ways to fit evolution and its billions-of-years time frame into the biblical account of creation. In essence, they want to continue to say that they believe in God and the Bible, but they also want to say that they believe in certain parts of evolution as well. They want to "have their cake and eat it, too." So the question arises: Can both the Bible and evolution be true?* Those who

---

* Standard definitions of evolution exclude God since they state that evolution is a **fully natural process** and that the Universe is self-contained (which means that it has not been created or acted upon by any outside force).

claim to believe in both evolution and the Bible generally are known as "theistic evolutionists." Theistic comes from the Greek *theos*, which means "God." Thus, theistic evolution is the view which suggests that God does exist, but that evolution is true, too. God simply used evolution to produce the Universe and its inhabitants.

The obvious place to start an investigation into this matter would be the introduction of the Bible—Genesis 1. The introduction of any sentence, story, or book is extremely important. For instance, if your mother really wants to get your attention, she likely will introduce the sentence with your name: "John Allen Thomas, you better straighten up!" Introductions are important because they often determine whether you decide to pay attention to the rest of the story. This is no less true of the introduction of the Bible. The first few chapters of Genesis tell the interesting and important story of the origin of the Universe.

The first two chapters of the Bible, for example, tell how God created the heavens and the Earth, and all of the animals, plants, and humans that existed. His creative activities lasted six consecutive days, and on the seventh day He rested from those activities. Exodus 20:11 sums it up like this: "For in six days the Lord made the heavens and the earth, the sea, and all that is in them, and rested the seventh day." The Bible states quite clearly that **everything** in the Universe, whether in the heavens or on the Earth, was created in six days. It is here that the Bible and evolution encounter their first major conflict. Evolution claims that everything in the Universe came into being by a gradual process that took billions of years, while the Bible says that it took only six days.

In order to fit evolutionary time into the Bible, billions of years must be inserted into the first few chapters of Genesis; without such vast stretches of time, evolution is impossible. But where and how can it be added to the biblical text? The fact of the matter is, there are only three possible places to insert the billions of years required by evolution: (1) **before** the creation week of Genesis; (2) **during** the creation week; or (3) **after** the creation week. Let's examine each of these options.

BEFORE THE CREATION WEEK: THE GAP THEORY

Through the years, people have searched for a way to place the time necessary for an ancient Earth **before** the creation week. The Gap Theory was proposed to do exactly that by suggesting that God's **original** creation of the world actually occurred in Genesis 1:1. It included a fully functional Earth complete with animals, plants, and even humans who lived before Adam. However, that creation (or so the theory goes) was destroyed as a result of Satan's disobedience and rebellion. The war between Satan and God supposedly was fought on Earth, and left this planet "without form and void" (Genesis 1:2). This would account for the billions of fossils found within the Earth, since they are the remnants of the "gap destruction." Beginning in Genesis 1:2, God then "re-created" the Earth in six literal, 24-hour periods.

While this may be a fascinating theory, it cannot possibly be true if the biblical record is taken at face value. First, where in the Bible do we read about any "original" creation having taken place prior to the one recorded in Genesis 1:1ff.? There is no such information provided within God's Word. Second, where do we read in the Bible about any "war" taking place **on the Earth** between Satan and God? Such an idea is not to be found within Scripture. Third, the Gap Theory blatantly contradicts Exodus 20:11: "For in six days the Lord made the heavens and the earth, the sea, and all that is in them, and rested the seventh day." If God made **everything** in six days, how many things did He make **before** those days? The answer, of course, is—**none!**

Fourth, the Gap Theory is false because it states that humans existed prior to Adam and Eve. Yet the inspired apostle Paul said that Adam was **the first man** (1 Corinthians 15:45) and that death entered this world as a direct result of Adam and Eve's sin (1 Corinthians 15:21; Romans 5:12; 8:20-22). If the Gap Theory is correct, a band of sinful people lived and died many years before Adam. The simple fact of the matter is, Paul and the Gap Theory cannot both be right.

DURING THE CREATION WEEK: THE DAY-AGE THEORY

Not everyone tries to insert time into the biblical text by using the Gap Theory. Some have argued that the "days" discussed in Genesis were not literal 24-hour periods, but instead were lengthy eons of time. After all, they say, the word translated "day" in Genesis 1 can have up to seven different meanings, and on rare occasions it even can refer to a long period of time.

So, how long were the days of the creation week, really? According to those who advocate the Day-Age Theory, the creation week was composed of long eons of time, each of which consisted of millions or billions of years. Could that be the case?

No. The author of Genesis wanted his readers to understand—in no uncertain terms—that the six days of creation were literal, 24-hour periods. Here are the reasons we know that. First, the writer defined the word "day" (Hebrew *yom*) by saying that it was composed of "an evening and a morning." Whenever that phrase is used with the word "day" in parts of the Old Testament that are not prophetic, it **always** means a 24-hour day—no exceptions.

Second, whenever a number comes before the word day in Old Testament non-prophetical literature like Genesis 1, it **always** means a literal, 24-hour period. Third, whenever the word "day" appears in the plural form (*yamim*) in the same type of literature, it **always** means a literal day. In fact, the Old Testament uses this word more than 700 times, and it always means a literal day in its non-prophetic uses. Thus, when Exodus 20:11 says: "For in six days (*yamim*) the Lord made the heavens and the earth," there can be absolutely no doubt that the text is speaking of six literal days.[*]

Fourth, the writer of Genesis had other ways of saying that the periods were long eons of time. He could have used the Hebrew word *dôr*, which means long periods of time, but he did not. Instead, he employed the word day, modified it with "evening and morning," put numerals before it, and made it plural (as in Exodus 20: 11 and 31:17). Moses used practically every means at his disposal to show that the days were **not** long peri-

[*] Morris, Henry (1970), *Biblical Cosmology in Modern Science* (Grand Rapids, MI: Baker).

ods of time, but instead were literal, 24-hour periods. Thus, the idea that billions of years needed for evolution might have occurred during the creation week simply cannot be defended.

But what about 2 Peter 3:8—"with the Lord one day is as a thousand years and a thousand years as one day"? Isn't this New Testament passage teaching that to God, a day is a very long time? The answer to this question is, "No, it is not." Let's take a look at the passage.

In 2 Peter 3:8, the apostle is not addressing the days of Genesis 1. If you begin reading in 2 Peter 3:1, you will notice that Peter was not talking about the week of creation, but was speaking of the "last days" when Christ will return. Some people said that Christ was taking too long to come back. Peter wanted his readers to understand that God is not bound by time. God can do more in a day than humans can do in a thousand years, or God may wait a thousand years to do what humans think He should do in a day.

It is interesting to note that God recognizes the difference between an earthly day and an earthly thousand years. It also is interesting to note that Peter did not say that a day **is** a thousand years or that a thousand years **is** a day. Instead, he stated that a day is **as** a thousand years, and a thousand years is **as** one day. God always has recognized the difference between an earthly day and a year. Genesis 1:14 is a good example of this, because God spoke of the Sun and Moon being useful to humans for "signs and for seasons, for **days** and for **years**." If the days of Genesis 1 are not 24-hour periods, but billions of years, then what would a "year" be? The passage in 2 Peter 3:8 shows that God is able to communicate the difference to human beings. And what, exactly, did He say the time periods in Genesis 1 were? **Days!**

AFTER THE CREATION WEEK

We have seen that the time needed for evolution to take place cannot be placed **during** the six days of creation because they were literal, 24-hour periods. We also have seen that the time cannot be placed **before** the six days of creation, because the Bible says that God created everything in six days. The only possible place left for the eons of time is **after** the creation week.

Some have suggested that perhaps Adam and Eve were in the Garden of Eden for many years before they sinned, and that vast amounts of time might be placed there. But Genesis 5:5 restricts the amount of time that Adam and Eve were in the Garden to a maximum of 930 years, since Adam died at that age. Furthermore, we know that "days" and "years" already were being counted before Adam and Eve sinned, because Genesis 1:14 uses both of those terms in a literal, everyday sense.

One other item needs to be discussed. It is extremely difficult to insert the time necessary for evolution **after** the creation week, since the biblical genealogies (which we discussed in the previous chapter) limit that time to a few thousand years. There simply is no room in the genealogies for millions (or billions) of years—which probably explains why very few people attempt to place the time necessary for an old Earth after the creation week.

Other equally false ideas have been suggested, but the material presented here, and in chapter 8, provides an airtight case which shows that the Earth is only about 6,000 years old. The billions of years required for evolution to have occurred find no place within the Bible.

CONCLUSION

Many theories have been concocted to allow people to believe in evolution and yet still try to maintain a belief in the Bible as God's Word. However, all of these theories fall short, and it soon becomes clear that **either** the Bible is true **or** evolution is true, **but they cannot both be true** since they teach contradictory concepts. A person cannot logically believe that the Bible is true, and then at the same time believe that evolution is true. It is an "either...or" proposition, not a "both...and." Remember, science books and theories are rewritten every few years, but "the Word of the Lord endures forever" (1 Peter 1:25).

DISCUSSION QUESTIONS

1. The Bible and evolution cannot both be true. Why? Some people say that both can be true, so how do they fit the two together?

2. According to the Gap Theory, what is responsible for many of the fossils found in the Earth? Where does the Gap Theory propose to fit the billions of years necessary for evolution to take place?

3. Numerous verses in the Bible can be used to refute false ideas like the Gap Theory. Which verse is one of the most damaging to the theories that attempt to fit evolution into the biblical account? Why?

4. What does the Day-Age Theory say? Sometimes 2 Peter 3:8 is used to try to justify this theory. Why will that not work? How does Genesis 1:14 fit into the discussion?

5. Why do you think that many people have tried to fit evolution into the Bible? Do you think it is due to the fact that the text of the Bible points them that way, or is it more likely because of what "current scientific theory" teaches? If God is all-powerful, why would He need to use evolution to create the Universe?

"For in six days the Lord made the heavens and the earth, the sea, and all that is in them, and rested on the seventh day."

Exodus 20:11

Dinosaurs often are the first battleground in a person's life where creation and evolution clash.

THE DINOSAUR DILEMMA

Small children flocked to the box office, accompanied, of course, by their willing parents, to buy tickets for one of Walt Disney's animated movies—*Dinosaur*. It seems that all a movie company has to do to make a load of money is plaster a picture of a creature like *Tyrannosaurus rex* on a poster and promise to make it the star of the show. From *Jurassic Park* to *Toy Story 2*, dinosaurs are thrust into the public gaze. But what in the world do dinosaurs have to do with a book on Christian evidences?

THE CONFLICT

Because dinosaurs grab the attention of both young and old alike, they are an extremely useful educational tool. Barney is nothing more than a big, purple dinosaur, yet thousands of small children sit mesmerized for hours on end by his lessons on life. Since dinosaurs are so popular, many evolutionists use them as an effective way to present evolution to children at a young age. If a child can be taught that dinosaurs lived hundreds of millions of years before mankind, then belief in the Bible and its account of Creation can be undermined. Dinosaurs often are the first battleground in a person's life where creation and evolution clash. Let's take a look at some of the main issues.

DID DINOSAURS REALLY LIVE ON THE EARTH?

In 1822, an English medical doctor by the name of Gideon Mantell, and his wife Mary Ann, set off in his horse and buggy to treat one of his patients. While Dr. Mantell attended the patient, Mrs. Mantell went for a stroll near a rock quarry, where she came across a pile of rocks beside the road. Looking closer at the rocks, she saw some huge fossil teeth. Knowing that her husband was an avid fossil collector, she rushed them back to him. After examining the fossils, they both walked back to the rock quarry and found several more teeth similar to the first. They showed them to some prominent scientists, but none could correctly identify the animal to which they once belonged. Dr. Mantell concluded that they must have belonged to a long-dead creature that was unlike anything still living.

By 1842, enough huge teeth and bones had been discovered by various people to cause scientist Richard Owen, head of the British Museum of Natural History in London, to conclude that a whole tribe of giant, lizard-like reptiles had lived in the past. He named them "dinosaurs"—from two Greek words meaning "terribly great lizards." Since that time, so many fossils of these magnificent creatures have been discovered that anyone who denies their existence has not looked carefully at the wealth of evidence. Make no mistake about it, dinosaurs did live!

When Did They Live?

When, exactly, did dinosaurs live? According to the theory of evolution, dinosaurs began to thrive about 175 million years ago. They "ruled" the Earth for over 100 million years, and became extinct about 65 million years ago. The ancestors of modern-day humans then evolved about four million years ago. Thus, according to evolutionary theory, dinosaurs and humans were separated by a period of 60 million years.

However, according to the biblical account of creation, all living creatures were fashioned on days five and six. Exodus 20:11 says: "For in six days the Lord made the heavens and the earth, the sea, and all that is in them." And, as we learned in chapter 8, the Bible teaches that the Earth is only about 6,000 years old. Thus, according to the Bible, dinosaurs could not have lived on this Earth much earlier than 6,000 years ago. Furthermore, the Bible plainly states that both man and the beasts of the Earth (including dinosaurs) were created on day six of the creation week (Genesis 1:24-31).

The Bible and evolution cannot be reconciled in this area. Evolution says that dinosaurs lived millions of years ago and never lived side-by-side with humans, while the Bible states that man was created about 6,000 years ago and lived at the same time as the dinosaurs. Only one of these two conclusions can be true. Which one is it? Let's look at the evidence.

Dinosaurs and Mankind:
Next-Door Neighbors?

In the early 1900s, an archaeologist named Dr. Samuel Hubbard was excavating some old Indian ruins in the Hava Supai section of the Grand Canyon in Arizona. On the walls of the canyon, he found drawings of many different animals, including an elephant, an ibex, and. . . a dinosaur! Near the drawings, he found fossilized dinosaur footprints preserved in rocks that were supposed to be 165 million years old. How would the Indians know how to draw such an accurate picture of a dinosaur that none of them had ever seen (or had described to them by someone who had seen it)? (Remember that dinosaurs were not even identified in modern times until the early 1800s, while the Indians who made these rock drawings lived many years before that.)

Another amazing discovery came from the hills of a small city in Mexico by the name of Acambaro, located below the El Toro mountains. In 1944, a German businessman by the name of Waldemar Julsrud accidentally stumbled upon over 30,000 ancient artifacts. These fascinating clay figurines depicted fish, humans, snakes, crocodiles, musical instruments, and numerous other things. The figurines date back to a civlization that flourished from approximately 800 B.C. to A.D. 200. Eighteen of the figurines were sent to the University of Pennsylania, where they were dated (using evolution-based dating methods) at 2,500 B.C. However, this date was later retracted when the university dating laboratory learned that, included among the figurines, were representations of dinosaurs.

Other finds verify the conclusion that the evolutionary timetable is completely inaccurate. Human footprints have been found repeatedly in layers that are supposed to be millions of years old. Dr. Albert G. Ingalls, an evolutionist, discovered human footprints in coal veins (supposedly about 250 million years old) in Kentucky, Virginia, Pennsylvania, and several other states. On another occasion, a trilobite fossil was found embedded in a human sandal print, which is astounding since evolutionists claim that trilobites were extinct almost 450 million years before humans ever existed.[*]

DINOSAURS: BOOK, CHAPTER, AND VERSE?

If dinosaurs really did live at the exact same time as humans, and if the Bible gives us an accurate history of the human race all the way back to Creation, then why is it that we don't read about dinosaurs anywhere in the Bible?

Even if dinosaurs never were mentioned in the Bible, that wouldn't mean that they did not exist, or that they existed millions of years before mankind. After all, the Bible never mentions bacteria or a duck-billed platypus, but we know that both exist.

The truth of the matter is that the Bible does mention animals that closely resemble the magnificent creatures we call dinosaurs. In Job 40, God described an animal that seems to fit perfectly the description of a dinosaur.

---

[*] Lammerts, Walter (1976), *Why Not Creation?* (Grand Rapids, MI: Baker), pp. 186-187.

The Behemoth

Job 40:15-24 describes a huge creature, the behemoth, that dwells near water, eats plants like an ox, has a tail that swings like a mighty cedar tree, and has huge bones like beams of bronze. Many have tried to say that this intriguing creature is an elephant or a hippopotamus. But a person does not have to be a zoologist to see that the tails of the elephant and the hippopotamus are tiny compared to huge cedars, some of which can grow to be over 120 feet tall. Truthfully, no animal matches the description of the behemoth better than a huge, herbivorous dinosaur like *Apatosaurus*, *Diplodocus*, or any number of other sauropod dinosaurs. Why distort the description to make it fit some animal (like the elephant or hippo) that it doesn't really describe—when there are several extinct animals that fit the description perfectly?

Leviathan

Leviathan, another amazing creature, is described in Job 41, and was indeed an astonishing animal. It had skin that could not be penetrated by harpoons, teeth that were huge and terrible, scales that could not be parted, smoke and fire that billowed from its mouth and nostrils, and an underbelly that was as sharp as pieces of broken pottery. Some say that this passage must be talking about a crocodile. But that cannot be the case, because a crocodile has a soft underbelly and does not breathe smoke and fire. In fact, the word "dragon" comes to mind after reading about leviathan! But dragons never really lived, did they? Surely no animal could spew fire out of its mouth?

First, we should remember that the historical (not mythical or legendary) literature of numerous countries speaks of smoke-belching, fire-breathing animals. This is true for China, Taiwan, Korea, Great Britain, and many others. In some cases, line drawings of the animals even accompany the written descriptions, providing a "picture" of what the people saw. Second, if an electric eel can produce 500 volts of static electricity that can kill a grown human being, if a two-hundred pound Komodo dragon can run as fast as a horse, and if a bombardier beetle can produce a chemical "bomb" that explodes from its body at 212°F, why is it so difficult to believe that an animal could breathe smoke and fire? The animal kingdom is filled with all kinds of weird and wondrous creatures that have traits even the most accomplished science fiction writer could not imagine. Yet the animals themselves are quite real—not fictitious.

WHAT HAPPENED TO THE DINOSAURS?

No one knows exactly what happened to the dinosaurs. In his book, *The Great Dinosaur Mystery and the Bible*, Paul Taylor has noted that there are over 25 different theories attempting to explain the extinction of the "terribly great lizards."[*] One theory suggests that a large comet struck the Earth and sent a huge amount of dirt into the air. That dirt (and smoke from worldwide fires) blocked the Sun's rays, caused temperatures to drop drastically, and resulted in the death of much of the Earth's vegetation. Since the dinosaurs could not func-

---

[*] Taylor, Paul (1989), *The Great Dinosaur Mystery and the Bible* (Colorado Springs, CO: Chariot Victor), pp. 22-23.

tion in the cold, and could not find enough to eat, they eventually died out. Another theory suggests that predators ate the eggs of the dinosaurs, sending them into extinction.

One possible explanation for the extinction of the dinosaurs involves the Flood of Noah. God destroyed every living creature on the land that was not taken into Noah's ark. Thousands of dinosaurs probably were killed in the Flood, and their bones were buried very quickly (which could help explain the mass graveyards of dinosaur bones that are found all over the world). After the Flood, the Earth would have been quite different, and the dinosaurs probably did not flourish like they had prior to the Flood due to a change in climate and food supply. We know that all of them did not become extinct immediately, because people who lived after the Flood (like Job or the American Indians) saw these fascinating creatures. Perhaps they became extinct because they could not find enough food, or because men hunted them too heavily. We simply don't know why the dinosaurs are extinct—and we probably never will.

CONCLUSION

Dinosaurs did exist. Of that fact there is absolutely no doubt. They did not, however, live millions of years before humans. According to the Bible, they were created by God on day six. Even scientific findings show that they lived alongside human beings. The descriptions of the animals in Job prove that huge creatures resembling dinosaurs existed on Earth at the same time as man. Furthermore, it is not difficult to believe that amazing creatures like dinosaurs coexisted with mankind when we consider the astonishing characteristics of existing animals such as the electric eel, the bombardier beetle, and the Komodo dragon.

Establishing the fact that dinosaurs lived at the same time as men shows that the evolutionists' ideas regarding the age of the Earth are off by hundreds of millions of years. What use is a theory that not only misses the bull's eye, but misses the target altogether?

DISCUSSION QUESTIONS

1. Why does this book on Christian evidences include information about dinosaurs? Name some places you have seen material on dinosaurs. Generally speaking, what is the target audience for this material?

2. How do we know that dinosaurs really lived? When do evolutionists say that dinosaurs lived? According to the Bible, when did dinosaurs live? Why is it important to know when dinosaurs lived?

3. Did dinosaurs ever live at the same time as humans? Give some evidence to support your answer. How would the theory of evolution be affected if dinosaurs and humans coexisted?

4. Look over Job chapters 39-41 and discuss some clues found in the text that allow us to know that the behemoth and leviathan were actual creatures. Who does the Bible say had the ability to kill these strong animals? Give at least one possible way that many of them could have been killed.

5. God used dinosaur-like animals in the book of Job to prove that He existed and is all-powerful. For the most part, what are dinosaurs being used to teach today? Use 2 Peter 3:16 to discuss this situation and how it relates to the Bible.

"For the king, before whom I also speak freely, knows these things; for I am convinced that none of these things escapes his attention, since this thing was not done in a corner."

Acts 26:26

Critics do not like having to admit it, but they cannot successfully deny the fact that Jesus had a greater impact on the world than any single life before or after.

JESUS CHRIST—FACT OR FAIRY TALE?

Most children and adults easily recognize the name of Jesus Christ. Many can even tell the story of His life. However, those same people also recognize such names as Peter Pan, Snow White, and Cinderella. And they can relate the "facts" of these fairy tales as well. Is Jesus of Nazareth a fictional character that deserves to be included in a list of mystifying magicians, daring dragon slayers, and flying boy heroes?

Some people say that Jesus is a myth—a legend Who never actually lived on the Earth. After all, it is true that we do not have one single book or letter written by Jesus Himself. And, of course, no one has produced any physical evidence (such as His body) to verify His existence. What evidence is available to prove that Jesus actually walked on this Earth?

HOSTILE TESTIMONY

Interestingly, the first type of records are commonly known as "hostile" sources. Hostile sources were written by people who disliked Jesus and His followers. Such men certainly did not want to further the efforts of Christ or cause people to believe in His existence. In fact, they rejected His teachings and often reviled Jesus and His followers. Therefore, when these sources speak about Him, no one can accuse them of "shading the facts" in Jesus' favor.

A man named Tacitus will be the first hostile witness called to the stand. He was born about A.D. 56 and died about A.D. 117. He was an upper-class Roman with a good education who held high governmental positions under several Roman emperors. He is most famous for writing *Annals*—a history of Rome written around the year A.D. 115. In the *Annals*, he told of the Great Fire of Rome, which occurred in A.D. 64. Nero, the Roman Emperor, was suspected by many of having ordered the city set on fire. Tacitus wrote:

> Nero fabricated scapegoats, and punished with every refinement the notoriously depraved Christians (as they were popularly called). Their originator, Christ, had been executed in Tiberius' reign by the governor of Judea, Pontius Pilatus. But in spite of this temporary setback the deadly superstition had broken out afresh, not only in Judea (where the mischief had started) but even in Rome.

Tacitus hated both Christians and the Founder of their religion, Christ. He therefore had nothing positive to say about what he referred to as a "deadly superstition." He did, however, **have something to say about it.** His testimony establishes beyond any reasonable doubt that the Christian religion was historically relevant, and that its originator was a verifiable historical figure so famous that He attracted the attention of even the Roman Emperor himself!

Additional hostile testimony comes from Suetonius, who wrote around the year A.D. 120. His writings form reliable pieces of historical evidence. Twice in his history book, Suetonius specifically mentioned Christ or His followers. He wrote, for example: "Because the Jews at Rome caused continuous disturbance at the instigation of Chrestus, he [Claudius] expelled them from the city" (note that in Acts 18:2 Luke mentioned this expulsion by Claudius). *Chrestus* is probably a misspelling of *Christos*, the Greek word for Messiah. Suetonius further commented: "Punishments were also inflicted on the Christians, a sect professing a new and mischievous religious belief." Again, it is clear that Suetonius and the Roman government had feelings of hatred toward Christ and His so-called "mischievous" band of rebels. It is equally clear that Suetonius (and, in fact, most of Rome) recognized that Christ was the noteworthy Founder of a historical religion.

Another Roman by the name of Pliny the Younger also provided hostile testimony to the life of Jesus. In a letter he wrote in approximately A.D. 110, he used the terms "Christian" or "Christians" seven times, and wrote the name "Christ" three times. It is undeniably the case that Christians, with Christ as their Founder, had multiplied in such a way as to draw the attention of the Emperor and his officials by the time of Pliny. After examining this kind of evidence, it is impossible to deny the fact that Jesus Christ was recognized as an actual, historical person.

Even a casual reader who glances over the testimony of the hostile Roman witnesses will be struck by the fact that these men did not portray Christ as the Son of God or the Savior of the world. They verbally stripped Him of His Sonship, denied His glory, and belittled His magnificence. They described Him to their contemporaries, and for posterity, as a mere man. Yet even though they were greatly mistaken about **Who** He was, they nevertheless documented **that** He was. And for that we are indebted to them.

TESTIMONY OF JESUS AMONG THE JEWS

Even though much of the hostile testimony regarding the existence of Jesus originated from witnesses within the Roman Empire, such testimony is not the only kind of hostile historical evidence available. The Mishnah was a book of Jewish legal tradition put together around the year A.D. 200. Jewish rabbis studied the Mishnah, and even wrote a body of commentary based upon it known as the Gemares. The Mishnah and Gemares are known collectively as the Talmud. The complete Talmud surfaced around A.D. 300. If a person as influential as Jesus had existed in the land of Palestine during the first century, surely the rabbis would have had **something** to say about him. Undoubtedly, a man who supposedly confronted the smartest religious leaders of His day—and won—would be named among the opinions of His fellow rabbis. One biblical expert, F.F. Bruce, declared:

> According to the earlier Rabbis whose opinions are recorded in these writings, Jesus of Nazareth was a transgressor in Israel, who practiced magic, scorned the words of the wise, led the people astray, and said that he had not come to destroy the law but to add to it. He was hanged on Passover Eve for heresy and misleading the people.

His disciples, of whom five are named, healed the sick in his name.[*]

First-century Judaism, in large part, refused to accept Jesus Christ as the Son of the God. Yet it did not refuse to accept Him as a historical man from a literal city known as Nazareth. Nor did it fail to record crucial facts about His life and death.

Josephus is another extremely important Jewish witness. The son of Mattathias, he was born into a Jewish upper-class family around A.D. 37, and received a good education. Around the year A.D. 94, he wrote *Antiquities of the Jews*. Twice in that volume, Jesus' name flowed from Josephus' pen. *Antiquities* 18:3:3 reads as follows:

> And there arose about this time Jesus, a wise man, if indeed we should call him a man; for he was a doer of marvelous deeds, a teacher of men who receive the truth with pleasure. He led away many Jews, and also Greeks. This man was the Christ. And when Pilate had condemned him to the cross on his impeachment by the chief men among us, those who had loved him at first did not cease; for he appeared to them on the third day alive again, the divine prophets having spoken these and thousands of other wonderful things about him: and even now the tribe of Christians, so named after him, has not yet died out.

In addition, in *Antiquities* 20:9:1, Josephus documented how Ananus brought before the Sanhedrin "a man named James, the brother of Jesus who was called the

---

[*] Bruce, F.F. (1953), *The New Testament Documents—Are They Reliable?* (Grand Rapids: MI: Eerdmans), p. 102.

Christ, and certain others. He accused them of having transgressed the law, and condemned them to be stoned to death." Although Josephus was not a Christian, and therefore had no reason to help the cause of Christ, he still included Jesus' name in his history book for one simple reason—Jesus was a real, historical person.

RELIABILITY OF THE
NEW TESTAMENT RECORDS

Although the above list of hostile and Jewish witnesses proves beyond the shadow of a doubt that Jesus actually lived, it is by no means the only historical evidence available. The Gospels (Matthew, Mark, Luke, and John), and the other 23 books that form the New Testament, provide more information about Jesus than any other source(s) available. But are these records high-quality historical evidence, or do they fall short when compared to other types of historical documentation?

The fact is, the New Testament enjoys far more historical documentation than any other volume ever known. There are only 643 copies of Homer's *Iliad*, which is undeniably the most famous book of ancient Greece. No one doubts the text of Julius Caesar's *Gallic Wars*, but we have only 10 copies of it, the earliest of which was made 1,000 years after it was written. We have only two manuscripts of Tacitus' *Histories and Annals* (one from the ninth century and one from the eleventh). The *History of Thucydides*, another well-known ancient work, is dependent upon only eight manuscripts, the oldest of which is dated about A.D. 900 (along with a few papyrus scraps dated at the beginning of the Christian era). Yet when we realize that over 5,350 Greek manuscripts of the New Testament have been found, we see that there is absolutely no comparison. The Gospels—Matthew, Mark, Luke, and John—were complete (or substantially complete) before A.D. 100, with many of the writings circulating 20-40 years before that. It is an **absolutely undisputed fact** that the New Testament has more historical verification on its side than any other ancient book in the history of the world. And that is no exaggeration.

CONCLUSION

When someone asks the question, "Is the life of Jesus Christ a historic event?," he or she must remember, as one scholar wrote: "If we maintain that the life of our Lord is not a historical event, we are landed in hopeless difficulties; in consistency, we shall have to give up all ancient history and deny that there ever was such an event as the assassination of Julius Caesar."

Critics do not like having to admit it, but they cannot successfully deny the fact that Jesus had a greater impact on the world than any single life before or after. Nor can they deny the fact that Jesus died at the hands of Pontius Pilate. While Paul was on trial before King Agrippa, he said to Festus: "For the king, before whom I also speak freely, knows these things; for I am convinced that none of these things escapes his attention, since this thing was not done in a corner" (Acts 26:26).

As the earliest Christians welcomed a full examination of the credentials of the message that they preached, so do we today. These credentials have been weighed in the balance and **not** found wanting. The simple fact of the matter is that Jesus Christ "became flesh and dwelt among us" (John 1:14).

DISCUSSION QUESTIONS

1. What kind of evidence does it take to prove that someone actually lived? If your birth certificate were destroyed, how could anyone 200 years in the future prove you ever existed? What more could have been done to prove that Jesus actually lived on the Earth?

2. If Jesus did not really live on this Earth, how would that affect the way you live (see 1 Corinthians 15:15-19)? Name some things that would not be here if Jesus had not lived. How would that have affected the behavior of the entire world for the past 2,000 years?

3. Why do the hostile witnesses add so much credibility to the life of Jesus? Even though the New Testament certainly is not hostile toward Christ, why is it trustworthy evidence of His life? How does the way that we date time fit into this discussion?

4. Name some things that normal people do that Jesus also would have done (think about His life as a carpenter, and the everyday chores He would have performed). What do passages like John 4:6 and John 11:35 show us about Jesus?

5. Read Hebrews 4:15 and Matthew 4:1-11 and discuss how this phrase uttered by many supervisors and bosses fits into the life of Jesus: "I will not ask my employees to do anything I won't do." If Christ never really lived on the Earth, what does that do to the Bible?

"And truly Jesus did many other signs in the presence of His disciples, which are not written in this book; but these are written that you may believe that Jesus is the Christ, the Son of God, and that believing you may have life in His name."

John 20:30-31

Once a person denies the greatest miracle of all—creation at the hand of God—then he or she is forced to deny that miracles of any kind can occur.

MIRACLES

A person cannot read many pages of the New Testament (or the Old Testament for that matter) without coming across a miracle. Miracles spatter the pages of the Bible like polka dots on a Dalmatian—the 10 plagues in Egypt, the healing of people with leprosy, the resurrection of dead people, the virgin birth, and numerous other amazing wonders. But Jesus of Nazareth goes down in history as the most famous miracle worker of all time. He fed thousands of people with a few small loaves and fishes that were intended to feed only one small boy. He raised people from the dead after their bodies already had begun to decay. And healing otherwise "incurable" lepers was a common practice for this great wonder worker. Yet many educated people today deny that miracles are real or possible. They maintain that the wonders performed by Jesus must have been fictitious, or must have had a purely natural explanation. Did Jesus and others in the Bible perform mighty miracles, or are the stories wishful thinking written by superstitious and unscientific fanatics?

WHAT IS A MIRACLE?

In order to decide if miracles actually occurred, we first must know the definition of a miracle. A miracle is an event that defies natural laws and that can be accounted for only by a supernatural explanation. For example, walking on a dirt road is not a miracle, but defying the law of gravity and walking on water is a miracle. Again, there is nothing extraordinary about reviving a person by using CPR, but there is something miraculous about raising a person who has been dead for several days. Genuine miracles may be accepted by some and rejected by others, but they usually draw some type of response from almost everyone.

SOME "JUST SAY NO" TO MIRACLES

Some people adamantly claim that **any** type of miracle is absolutely impossible. Why do they say "no" to miracles? There are numerous reasons, but perhaps the most important is that they do not believe that God exists (or if He does, He does not intervene in the natural world). A person who believes that the Universe and all living things evolved through natural processes over billions of years cannot believe in miracles, because he or she thinks that there is nothing outside of nature. Since a miracle is an event that has only a supernatural explanation, no such event could ever occur in a world where only natural forces operate. Once a person denies the greatest miracle of all—creation at the hand of God—then he or she is forced to deny that miracles of any kind can occur.

These people are correct about one thing: If God does not exist (or if He does but is unwilling to intervene in His creation) then miracles cannot occur. On the other hand, if God does exist (and chapters 1 and 2 of this book argue convincingly that He does!), then miracles are possible. It makes perfectly good sense to conclude that if this Universe was created, then the Creator occasionally would intervene through miracles to accomplish His purposes.

God Wouldn't Break the Law

Another idea suggests that God did create the Universe, but that His activities stopped at creation. Therefore, He no longer intervenes in this world through miracles, because that would break the natural laws He established at the time of creation.

The problem with this idea is that it does not consider the fact that the natural laws do not apply to God since He is not a natural being. The Laws of nature cannot be "broken." For instance, the First Law of Thermodynamics states that matter or energy can be neither created nor destroyed **in nature.** The two words "in nature" must be included for the statement of the Law to be worded correctly. Nothing in nature—man, beast, or matter—can break this Law. No scientists, regardless of how smart they become, ever will be able to create matter or energy —the law is impossible to break. However, since God is not part of nature, the Law does not apply to Him.

To illustrate, think of the Universe as one room. God established natural laws that apply to everything in that room, and then He locked the door. It is impossible for matter or energy to be created or destroyed in that room. But, now suppose that God unlocks the door and puts another chair in the room or takes a chair out of the room. Did God break the law He established in the room? No, because everything in the room (Universe) still functions according to the natural laws, but since God is outside of the room then the laws do not apply to Him.

THE MIRACLES OF JESUS

Undoubtedly, Jesus Christ maintains the title as the most famous miracle Worker of all time. The Gospels tell how Jesus roamed the countryside in Palestine healing the sick, raising the dead, and causing the blind to see. His fame for doing miracles even reached the official ears of Herod, who "hoped to see some miracle done by Him" (Luke 23:8). Josephus, a Jew who was by no means a Christian, wrote that Jesus was "a doer of marvelous deeds." Other Jewish rabbis who hated Jesus said that he practiced "sorcery" or "magical arts." His enemies needed to call His deeds either sorceries or magical arts because the works obviously were not normal and could not be performed by others.

Why Did Jesus Perform Miracles?

In John 20:31, we read why Jesus performed miracles —so "that you may believe that Jesus is the Christ, the Son of God, and that believing you may have life in his name." The miracles of Christ recorded in the Gospels show that Jesus had been given all power in Heaven and on Earth. Trustworthy men documented that He had power over the human body, and could heal sickness and disease with the gentle touch of His hand or a kind word from His mouth (Matthew 8:1-4). On other occasions, He proved that He had power over the spiritual world by forgiving sins (Luke 5:20-24) and casting out demons (Luke 6:18). He also had power to control the physical world by calming storms and walking on water (Matthew 14:25-33). And His power over death was documented through His glorious resurrection three days after his crucifixion (John 20:24-29).

Jesus' miracles were designed to prove that He was the Son of God. Even the Pharisees, His worst enemies, admitted: "This man works many signs. If we let Him alone like this, everyone will believe in Him" (John 11:47-48). But they still refused to believe that He was God's Son. Many of them saw Him raise Lazarus from the dead, heal the sick, and cause the blind to see. They even had proof that He rose from the dead, yet they would not accept Him as the Son of God.

Why should it be any different today? Anyone who examines the evidence should be able to see that this world must have had a Creator. The Bible is inspired by that Creator, and informs us that Jesus performed miracles to prove He was the Son of God. Yet many people will brush aside all the evidence, just as the Pharisees did, and deny Jesus' deity. The Judgment Day will find those people hearing the words of Christ: "Woe to you! ...For if the mighty works which were done in you had been done in Tyre and Sidon, they would have repented long ago in sackcloth and ashes" (Matthew 11:21).

CONCLUSION

Miracles are only impossible in a world with no God. In the past, God used miracles to create the Universe and to provide credibility for the men who had been entrusted with His message. Jesus repeatedly performed miraculous deeds in order to prove to His followers (and to His enemies) that He was the Son of God. Sadly, many people during Christ's day refused to believe in Him as God's Son. And just as sadly, many today stubbornly refuse to believe in the Sonship of Christ. As He told the unbelieving Pharisees of His day, so will He tell the modern day disbelievers, "Woe to you!

DISCUSSION QUESTIONS

1. What did miracles prove about the ones who could do them? Use John 9:32-33 and other passages to formulate your answer. Why does the Bible document so many miracles?

2. In the Bible, miracles are recorded in factual terms just like historical and geographical information. Since the Bible has been proven time and again to be correct in its historical and geographical information, what does that say about its information on miracles?

3. What would you say is the biggest obstacle to believing in biblical miracles? Why are miracles believable once this obstacle is removed?

4. Some people today believe that they can perform miracles like Jesus and His apostles did. Use Acts 8:17-18, 1 Corinthians 13:8, and James 1:25 to formulate an answer to this idea.

5. By using miracles, Jesus showed that He had power over which areas of life on this Earth? What were these miracles designed to do (read John 20:24-31)? List some miracles that will happen in the future (1 Peter 3:10-13, 1 Corinthians 15, etc.).

"He is not here; for He is risen, as He said. Come, see the place where the Lord lay."

Matthew 28:6

Peter boldly stated the truth of the matter almost 2,000 years ago: "This Jesus God has raised up, of which we are all witnesses" (Acts 2:32).

THE RESURRECTION OF JESUS CHRIST

Imagine sitting in McDonald's munching on some hot fries and a Big Mac®. Suddenly, a rather ordinary man stands up and demands everyone's attention. He claims that in January 2001, one of his good friends died, was buried for three days, and rose again. Further, the man says that everyone listening should drop everything to spread the news of this amazing miracle. What would you do? You probably would finish your burger, throw away your trash, and go about your everyday activities —thinking that the man was "one brick shy of a load."

But now let us suppose that you are in Bible class, and the teacher declares that Jesus Christ died, was buried for three days, and rose again. What makes the story of Jesus any different from the one proclaimed at the McDonald's? Why should a person believe that Jesus Christ rose from the dead?

THE FACTS SUPPORT THE CLAIM

One of the most amazing characteristics of the New Testament is the complete trustworthiness of its checkable facts such as ancient city locations and names of governmental officials. The late Nelson Glueck, a highly respected archaeologist, once said that no archaeological discovery ever had contradicted the Bible. And, he went on to point out, hundreds of such discoveries have confirmed the Bible even in the smallest details. Whenever biblical statements and events are compared with historical or archaeological **facts**, the two always stand in complete harmony with one another. Because the New Testament exhibits this kind of phenomenal accuracy, we should be willing to give it the same respect we give any other reliable source of information.

EVIDENCE SUPPORTING THE RESURRECTION

In order to verify that Jesus actually rose from the dead, we must provide accurate, factual information that cannot be disproved. The remainder of this chapter will present such evidence.

The Event Foretold

King David, about a thousand years before Jesus ever walked on the Earth, explained that Christ would die and rise again. In Psalm 16:10, David prophesied of Jesus when he wrote: "For You will not leave my soul in Hades, nor will You allow Your Holy One to see corruption." Peter quoted this verse in Acts 2:27 to prove that the Old Testament had foretold the resurrection of Jesus.

Jesus added weight to this prophecy when He declared, on several different occasions, that He would die and be resurrected. He said that the Jews would destroy the temple of His body, but that He would raise it up in three days (John 2:19). On another occasion, Jesus proclaimed that just as Jonah was in the belly of the fish for three days and three nights, He would be in the "heart of the Earth" for the same amount of time (Matthew 12:38-40). And if that were not clear enough, Mark 8:31-32 records that He openly declared that the Jewish leaders would kill Him, but after three days He would rise again.

Jesus made the point so clear that even the stubborn Pharisees could not miss it. In Matthew 27:63, when they persuaded Pilate to place a Roman guard at the tomb, they quoted Jesus' saying, "After three days I will rise." They knew exactly what Jesus had said He would do, and they did everything in their power to stop it. But "everything in their power" was not enough to hinder God's plan for Jesus' resurrection—an event that David had prophesied a thousand years earlier.

An Empty Tomb

The fact that Jesus' tomb was empty cannot be denied. In Acts 2, Peter stood before more than 3,000 people in the middle of Jerusalem and boldly proclaimed that the tomb where Jesus had been laid was empty. All the Jewish leaders needed to do to defeat the apostle's teaching was produce the body of Jesus. The tomb was within walking distance, and Peter was making an open challenge.

The Jewish leaders, however, could not refute the fact that the tomb was empty. Instead, they were forced to fabricate the lie that Christ's disciples stole His body while the guards slept (Matthew 28:13). Their attempt at deception, however, was doomed to fail, because most guards who fell asleep at their posts were subject to death (Acts 12:19). Furthermore, if the soldiers really were asleep, how would they know who took the body? And how could the soldiers sleep through all the noise of rolling the large stone away from the entrance of the tomb? Not only were the Jews unable to disprove the empty tomb, but they actually **verified** its emptiness with their lie.

From Fear to Faith

The night Jesus was arrested in Gethsemane was a bleak time for His disciples. Just hours before the arrest, they had boldly promised to die with their Lord. Yet when the moment came for them to lay down their lives, they scurried away in fear. Even "bold" Peter denied the Lord three times! The disciples were scared for their lives, disillusioned by their dashed hopes for a kingdom that did not come, and running from anyone who might connect them with Jesus of Nazareth.

But only a few weeks after their timid acts of cowardice, they stood together in defiance of Jewish authorities and proclaimed that Jesus was the promised Messiah Who had risen from the grave. No amount of beatings, lashings, imprisonment, or threatening could stop them from preaching about the resurrection (Acts 4:18-20). Even Saul, the young Pharisee who had dedicated his life to torturing and killing Christians, became an avid defender of the resurrection (1 Corinthians 15:4). James died because of his dedication to the resurrection (Acts 12:2), and tradition indicates that every one of the other apostles, except John, met a similar martyr's fate.

What event could change a band of frightened doubters into a host of powerful preachers? What could cause these men to jeopardize their lives and the lives of their families? Some have suggested that the apostles concocted the resurrection story and pawned it off on humanity as the truth. But it is ridiculous to believe that these men would suffer such agony to propagate something they knew to be a lie. Truth be told, only one thing could be the driving force behind the disciples' change of heart. Peter said it well: "This Jesus God has raised up, of which we are all witnesses" (Acts 2:32).

Testimony of Women

In first-century Israel, women certainly did not enjoy the rights, freedoms, privileges, or respect that they do today. One Hebrew poem that circulated during New Testament times (but that is not found in the Bible) went like this: "Blessed art thou, O Lord our God, King of the universe, who hast not made me a Gentile (heathen). Blessed art thou, O Lord our God, King of the universe, who hast not made me a slave. Blessed art thou, O Lord our God, King of the universe, who hast not made me a woman." Matthew 14:21 documents the fact that often, women and children were not even considered important enough to count. History tells us that the testimony of women was worth very little in a first-century court.

Therefore, if a person wanted to present a case to prove or disprove something to a first-century Jewish audience, one of the last places he would look for witnesses was among women. Yet, when the story of Jesus' resurrection began to surface, the star witnesses were women (Matthew 28:5-8). Why would the gospel writers use women as witnesses if they were trying to convince a skeptical first-century audience? There is only one good answer: as eyewitnesses to the resurrected Lord, they were telling the truth.

Ask Them Yourself

Many people in the first century did not believe that Christ rose from the dead. They denied that such a resurrection was possible, and they cast suspicion on any story mentioning such a thing. For this reason, New Testament writers included the strongest evidence available for any case—honest eyewitnesses. Even today the testimony of multiple, honest eyewitnesses carries substantial weight in any case. What better evidence is there than a host of human eyewitnesses?

The modern-day skeptic might suggest that a photograph, VHS video, or DVD of the event would be much more weighty than human testimony. But consider this: photographs of the event would not be sufficient, because they easily can be altered and distorted. A video or DVD certainly could be "doctored" to produce almost any story desired. Photographs and movies show many things that look exactly like real life due to amazing advances in technology. However, we learned early in life "not to believe everything we see on TV." If an actual event in history ever could be proved, it would take human eyewitnesses to do it. And that is exactly what God provided.

In 1 Corinthians 15:5-8, Paul declared that Jesus had been seen by Peter and James, and "over five hundred brethren at once." But he did not stop there. Rather, he went on to state that "the greater part remain to the present, but some have fallen asleep." Paul simply was saying that there were several hundred people still alive at the time he wrote his epistle who had seen the resurrected Christ with their own eyes. The apostle invited his readers—if they didn't trust him—to ask Peter, James, or the hundreds of others who had seen Jesus after He was raised from the dead.

WHAT DOES IT MATTER?

Belief in the resurrection of Jesus of Nazareth was so important to the early church that Paul proclaimed: "If Christ is not risen, then our preaching is vain and your faith is also vain.... And if Christ is not risen, your faith is futile; you are still in your sins!" (1 Corinthians 15: 14,17). The central theme of Peter's sermon in Acts 2 was that Christ's tomb was empty because He had been resurrected. When Paul preached to the pagans on Mars Hill in Acts 17, one of his key points to the Athenians was that God would judge the world through Jesus Christ, Whom He had raised from the dead.

The church of our Lord spread like wildfire in Palestine and throughout the entire world. One message caused millions of people to change their hearts and lives—Jesus Christ had been resurrected and was alive and well. If Christ did not rise from the grave, how can anyone explain the fact that the church, which was constructed on the foundation of His resurrection, spread around the globe? If Christ did not rise, how can the trustworthy message of so many credible witnesses be explained? If Christ did not rise, why would His followers gladly accept excruciating torture and eventual death to defend a lie? Peter boldly stated the truth of the matter almost 2,000 years ago: "This Jesus God has raised up, of which we are all witnesses" (Acts 2:32).

DISCUSSION QUESTIONS

1. Sometimes the gospel accounts of the resurrection seem to say things differently. How does this fact add credibility to the accounts, instead of detracting from them? Defining the word "collusion" will help answer this question.

2. Some people think that Jesus never really died at all, but only fainted or swooned. Discuss the evidence that shows this could not have been the case. How do verses like Mark 15:42-45 and Matthew 27:60 enter into the discussion?

3. One skeptic stated that he did not believe in the resurrection of Christ, and that in order to do so he would have to "draw up a 'wish list' of evidences" as follows:

* Perhaps a doctor's certificate of death.
* Contemporary interviews with people who saw such a body.
* Videos of the body entering a locked room.
* Documentary evidence that the room was actually locked.
* Appearances of this body in public places, say the Temple, or Pilate's palace."

This same man went on to say: "While I, personally, would be convinced by those evidences, plenty of people would demand even more proof of such an astonishing event as a resurrection."* Explain how all of his "wish list" items except one have been fulfilled. Also discuss why the one unfilled item would not provide very good evidence.

---

* Carr, Steven (no date), "The Resurrection," [On-line], URL: http://www.bowness.demon.co.uk/resr.htm

4. Paul stated in 1 Corinthians 15:20 that Jesus became the "firstfruits" of the dead. John wrote in Revelation 1:5 that He was "the firstborn from the dead." However, we read about others who rose from the dead before Jesus (1 Kings 17:22; John 11:43-44; Mark 5:39-43). Why, then, was Christ referred to as the "firstfruits" and "first-born" of the dead?

5. Where is Jesus now? What is He doing? What will He do in the future? Discuss verses that verify your answers.

AFTERWORD

Maturing into a young adult is tough. Dating, fitting in at school, playing sports, and studying are on the minds of teenagers everyday. "What will she say if I talk to her?" "Will I get to start in the next basketball game?" "Why don't my parents understand me?" "Should I drink this?" "Should I smoke that?" "How far is too far?" These, and other questions like them, fill the hearts and minds of young people all over the world.

But somewhere deep inside every one of us is a single, more important question. It doesn't surface all that often, and even when it does we often thrust it to the back of our mind so we aren't forced to deal with it. But sooner or later—whether we are 80 years old and dying of cancer, or sitting, unseatbelted, in a car doing flips into a ditch while wondering if we will live through the car wreck—we all must answer the question, "What will happen to me when I die?"

The material discussed up to this point in this book has provided ample evidence to establish the fact that God exists, the Bible is His Word, and Jesus Christ died and was resurrected from the grave. But so what! What does that have to do with the average teenage guy or girl who has been studying this book for the last several weeks?

Think with me for a moment. If there is a God Who went to all of the trouble of communicating His will in the Bible, then there must be something that He wants humans to do. What is it? What does God want a teenager in the 21st century to do with his or her life?

Before you go any further, you need to understand that what you are about to read is very simple to say but very difficult to do. It is like saying all you have to do to be a quarterback in the NFL is throw a football better than everyone else, or all you have to do to win the Olympics is run faster than everyone else. Two or three pages of a short book can explain what God wants you to do, but it takes a lifetime of dedication, determination, and self-control to be what He wants you to be.

But don't let words like dedication, determination, and hard work scare you. Everything worthwhile requires effort. Good grades never "crept" onto a person's report card while that person spent every day watching television; baseball or football skills never fell into someone's lap without hours of difficult practice; and a fulfilled, happy life with a secure final destination in heaven will not be easy to obtain. Jesus explained that the road to heaven is difficult, and only a few find it (Matthew 7:14).

So, what does God want from you? First, He simply wants you to hear His message (Romans 10:14). Truth always has been able to stand on its own, and God's message is pure truth. He does not want you to hear a watered-down version of His message, but the whole truth—so that you can have a fair chance to decide what to believe.

After you have heard the truth from God's inspired Word, He wants you to believe it. He has given us **more than enough** evidence to show that He is real, that His Word is true, and that His Son lived on Earth, died, rose again, and one day will come back to claim His faithful followers. Belief in God and His Word is not a blind "leap of faith" based on shaky evidence and irrational "religious" thinking. On the contrary, it is a reasonable conclusion based on trustworthy evidence. This belief, which also is known as faith, never comes as a result of "leaping" into accepting things without evidence. Instead, it comes through looking closely at the **facts**, and then using them to make wise decisions (Acts 8:37; 15:7; Romans 10:9).

Now the water starts to get deeper, and the hill starts to get more difficult to climb. After hearing the Word and believing it, God wants you to repent of your sins (Acts 2:38; Acts 17:30). The word "repent" means to stop doing what is wrong and start doing what is right. It includes godly sorrow and a change in attitude that results in a change of action. If a young man is having premarital sex with his girlfriend, then in order to repent he must be genuinely sorry for his sin and stop engaging in premarital sex. If a person has a filthy mouth, in order to repent he or she must be genuinely sorry and stop using such language. Repentance is one step in God's plan of salvation that many people refuse to take. Why is this the case? Apparently, they do not want to leave behind their lives of sin in order to follow God. Some of you reading this may be forced to decide, before the next weekend arrives, if you will repent of those sins that have separated you from God, and then start doing right.

Once we have repented, then we are ready to tell someone verbally about our belief in Christ. In Acts 8:37, the Ethiopian eunuch boldly remarked: "I believe that Jesus Christ is the Son of God." In the first century, many people were put to death for uttering that simple phrase. In the twenty-first century, it carries no less weight. By confessing Jesus as the Son of God and as Lord and Savior, we admit to our fellow men that we have stopped living for ourselves and started living for the Lord. The importance of confessing the Lord with our mouths cannot be overstated. The apostle Paul observed: "With the mouth confession is made to salvation" (Romans 10:10). But please understand that confessing Christ as your Lord is not "a one-time thing." Every day for the rest of your life, by your actions as well as your words, you should shout that He is Lord. And if the day ever should come that someone who is pressing a cold gun barrel against your temple demands that you deny your belief in Christ, the final words from your mouth should be "I believe that Jesus Christ is the Son of God."

After confessing your belief in Jesus, you have one simple, yet profound step to take in order to be a child of God. You must be baptized for the forgiveness of your sins (Acts 2:38; Mark 16:16; 1 Peter 3:21). To be baptized means to be totally immersed or dipped under water. It is sad that so many people today have neglected to teach that baptism is necessary for a person's salvation. In the book of Acts, when we read about people being saved, we learn that baptism was an essential part of their conversion. In Acts 22:16, for example, Saul was commanded to be baptized in order to "wash away" his sins.

Baptism is critically important because through it we contact the blood of Christ that forgives us of our sins. Paul put it this way: "Or do you not know that as many of us as were baptized into Christ Jesus were baptized into His death? Therefore we were buried with Him through baptism into death, that just as Christ was raised from the dead by the glory of the Father, even so we also should walk in newness of life" (Romans 6:3-4). Just as Christ died, was buried, and rose from the dead, when we are baptized we "die" to sin, are buried in water, and rise to live a new life as a Christian. Baptism is one of the most beautiful symbolic acts of all time. If a person leaves this simple step out of his life, then he has missed an essential element of salvation that God has communicated through His Word. Furthermore, when a person is immersed in water for the forgiveness of his or her sins, then God adds that person to the Lord's church, and his or her name is written clearly in God's Book of Life (Acts 2:47; Revelation 20:15).

As a new Christian, the Lord equips us with all that we need to remain faithful to Him. He never will allow us to be tempted beyond what we can handle, and He always will provide for us a way to escape from the devil (1 Corinthians 10:13). Although living a faithful Christian life can be tough, we will be able to accomplish all things through Christ Who gives us strength (Philippians 4:13). We can live forgiven and guilt-free, and know, without a doubt, that we are saved (1 John 5:13).